Heart Whispers From the Old Testament

by

Mary McLeary

Forward by Don McLeary

Living a Christian life means daily drawing closer to God and helping others do the same. As parents, Mary and I wanted our children to see us live our faith, and we prayed that they too would give their hearts to Him. Thankfully, each of our daughters and sons-in-law have that personal relationship with the Lord, and so do each of our grandchildren.

Leaving a spiritual heritage was also important to Mary's mother. Her journals provided the inspiration for Mary's first book, *In My Mother's Words*, and now *Heart Whispers from the Old Testament* adds to that inheritance.

Heart Whispers from the Old Testament reminds the reader that God has always spoken to people who took time to listen. Today's world is just as lost as it was centuries ago and God always found someone who magnified and glorified Him in terrible times.

Looking back to the Old Testament scriptures provides examples of how to live, yet always reminds us that though good examples are important, what the world really needed was a Savior.

That Savior is Jesus Christ. If you don't know Him, I pray He woos you through His Word. If you do know Him, I pray that reading Mary's book encourages you to magnify and glorify Him every day.

Thoughts about *Heart Whispers from the Old Testament*

The book of wisdom tells us twice "not to forsake the teaching of our mothers". Mary, not only did not forsake her mother's teaching, but she applied it to her own life and then shared it with the rest of us as well! What a blessing!

Carol Bivens – Sunday School and Bible Study Teacher

This book, like Mary's first book *In My Mother's Words,* is encouraging and comforting. When I am restless in the middle of the night, I can always depend on Mary's writings to make me feel like I've had a visit with my best friend."

Sue Gwathmey – Public School Librarian/Teacher

You can hear the heart of Mary McLeary in her devotional book *Heart Whispers from the Old Testament.* Her heart is devoted to Jesus Christ. She wrote this book with her grandchildren in mind, and that makes me smile because my three kids call her "Meme."

Scott Stidham – Sunday School Teacher and Head Football Coach at South Gibson County High School

Dedicated

To Matt a very special son, and Don, the love of my life; our daughters, Stacy and Holly and their husbands Scott and Wendell; our grandchildren: Landry, Nolan, Nash, Brandon and Maston.

You are joys beyond measure.

Preface

After opening Mother's present to me on her last Christmas, I became the keeper of journals full of wisdom whispered to her heart as she prayed and studied the Bible.

Her gift inspired a blog and eventually my first book *In My Mother's Words,* a compilation of family faith stories and entries from her journals.

Last year I started reading through the Bible and never got past the Old Testament. With each chapter, God whispered, "I'm in control," as he left a scripture on my heart along with thoughts I wanted to share with my grandchildren.

I wrote these down and then went back and found entries to add from Mother's prayer journals. When I began typing the daily thoughts, I added prayer prompts.

Heart Whispers from the Old Testament was written with my grandchildren in mind. Because God in His perfection never changes, the Spirit whispers comfort, hope, peace, and courage to our hearts now as He did thousands of years ago.

Dear Lord, Thank you for your Word that is always relevant. Bless each person who reads this book and make them wise as they seek Your will. Amen

FCA Camp at Black Mountain, NC

Recently we made a road trip to the mountains and were welcomed with cool temperatures and refreshing showers that provided nice changes from the humid nineties back home.

These mountains hold special memories for my husband so after checking into our hotel, we drove up a lush mountain road to the YMCA campus that also hosts summer camps for Fellowship of Christian Athletes.

Established in 1954, FCA has encouraged coaches and athletes to impact the world for Christ. It reaches over two million people annually on all levels of athletics and focuses on serving Christ through relationships and in the fellowship of the church.

FCA camps are a time for coaches and athletes to reach their potential by offering comprehensive athletic, spiritual and leadership training and focusing on integrity, serving, teamwork and excellence.

In the summer of 1965, an anonymous donor made it possible for an upcoming high school senior to attend an FCA camp. The life changing experience was reflected in the letter I received from my then high school sweetheart:

"Before I came to this conference, I lived my life only within myself. After listening to testimonies by men so admired in athletics, I found I no longer face life alone. I can share my problems with my personal friend and savior. I now have tremendous faith in God and His will for my life."

After a stellar senior year in high school this young man went on to be a part of two SEC championship teams and one National Championship team. He coached for nearly thirty years and returned to several FCA camps as a counselor.

Driving back up that mountain so many years later brought back memories of football games played in the open fields with other student athletes and testimonies given by famous speakers. Billy Graham, who was in his prime, came over one night to visit the campers.

On our way back home we followed a winding stream that flows at the bottom of the Great Smokey Mountains. As the water rushed over rocks and parted for the giant boulders lying in its path, I remembered the scripture in Psalms 62:7.

God is a mighty rock, my refuge.

In her journal Mother wrote, **"It is our responsibility to do all we can do to keep the gospel message alive for the next generation."**

We never found out who the anonymous donor was, but he provided the opportunity to begin building a life on The Mighty Rock.

Judges 6:37

Then Gideon said to God, "Look, I shall put a fleece of wool on the threshing floor; if there is dew on the fleece only, and it is dry on all the ground, then I shall know that You will save Israel by my hand, as you have said."

Gideon was a brave and godly young man who is listed as one of the heroes of the Old Testament.

When God chose Gideon for an important task, Gideon responded in verse 37 by "putting out the fleece".

In essence Gideon said, "God I will do what You ask if you will do this for me."

God did what Gideon asked and Gideon had the nerve to put out another fleece! God's patience overcame Gideon's doubts, but testing Him is not the best way to answer His call. An unquestioning faith will develop as our relationship to Him grows.

In her journal Mother wrote, **"Putting out the fleece is a poor decision-making method. Those who do this put limitations on God. Don't let a "fleece" become a substitute for God's wisdom that comes through Bible study and prayer."**

Dear Lord, Thank you for being patient with us, even when we question you. Help us to grow in faith so that we don't need to put out a fleece. Amen

Joshua 23:10

One man of you shall chase a thousand, for the Lord your God is He who fights for you, as He has promised you.

When an underdog in a sporting event fights hard and gives his/her opponent a scare, it is called a moral victory. He/she fought the good fight and came out a winner of sorts.

If a person takes an unpopular stand against overwhelming odds and doesn't get demolished in the process, that is also a moral victory.

A teenager who lives her faith may lose popularity, but her witness through the years could impact thousands.

In her journal Mother wrote, **"Victory depends not on strength or numbers but on obedience and commitment to Him."**

Heavenly Father, I thank you for strength when the odds are against us. Help us to have the courage to do whatever You ask us to do. Amen

Psalm 46:1

God is our refuge and strength a very present help in trouble.

My dad could play the piano, make wonderful Italian spaghetti and tell funny stories about his experiences during WWII. His work allowed him to be home on many week days so he often did the grocery shopping and ran the vacuum. He also took my brother and me to our various lessons and practices.

I never thought of him as a hero until I started reading about the fighting in North Africa during the war. As a Staff Sergeant in the Army Air Corp, I'm sure he and those he served with were expected to do heroic tasks.

God gave a regular guy the courage needed during the troubles of war. God will give us extra portions of bravery when we need it.

In her journal Mother wrote, **"Heroes in battle are not always heroes in daily life."**

Dear Lord, I thank you for those in all branches of the military who protect us. Give them courage when they need it, and help each of us live heroically for You. Amen

2 Samuel 11:2

Then it happened one evening that David arose from his bed and walked on the roof of the king's house. And from the roof he saw a woman bathing, and the woman was very beautiful.

The beautiful woman was Bathsheba who was the wife of Uriah, a soldier in King David's army. This verse is the beginning of a story full of sadness. His love for her resulted in Uriah's death (which David orchestrated) and the birth of a child who eventually died.

When I read this story, I always feel sorry for Bathsheba because, really, who says no to a king. Apparently he couldn't get the thought of her out of his mind, and (in my opinion) she paid a steep price for his attraction. David also lived with the consequences of his actions.

In her journal Mother wrote, **"No matter who you are, moral laxness will cause problems."**

Dear Lord, Thank you for giving us free will, but help us stay close to you so that our choices don't hurt others and displease you. Amen

Deuteronomy 30:19

. . I have set before you life and death, blessing and cursing. Therefore choose life that you and your descendants may live.

Satan is a liar. He will seek to discourage you and make you doubt yourself. Everyday wake up and bind him in Jesus name.

Pray for wisdom to see the truth when you must make a difficult choice. Your life and the lives of future generations might depend on a choice you make today.

In her journal Mother wrote, **"Just because you have won a single battle with temptations, does not mean you will automatically win the next one. We need to be constantly watchful against temptations. Sometimes Satan's strongest attacks come after a victory."**

Dear Lord, I thank you that Jesus chose to follow you all the way to the cross when He could have sold out to the devil. Help me remember that the enemy never quits trying to destroy me with his lies. Amen

Ecclesiastes 5:2-3

Do not be quick with your mouth. Do not be hasty in your heart to utter anything before God for God is in heaven, and you are on earth. Therefore let your words be few for a dream comes through much activity and a fool's voice is known by his many words.

I read in the newspaper today that a fifteen year old shot another teen over an argument they had earlier in the day. Apparently rash words were spoken and caused disaster.

The scripture tells us to turn the other cheek, and with guns being accessible to so many, I realize it is healthier to take a punch on both cheeks than risk being shot.

Maybe if we realized God hears every word uttered, we would be more careful in our conversations.

In her journal Mother wrote, **"Let us learn from the examples in God's word not to make rash vows."**

Dear Lord, Protect those you have given me to love. Make them cautious with their words and strong enough to turn the other cheek rather than speak hasty words they will regret. Amen

2 Chronicles 1:10

"Now give me wisdom and knowledge, that I may go out and come in before this people; for who can judge this great people of Yours?"

I know a teacher who questioned the wisdom of her newly hired principal so at the first opportunity she took another position. She told me later, "I don't claim to be the brightest bulb in the box, but I want my boss to be the brightest."

Power goes to those in leadership positions. The only way to lead effectively is to ask Him for guidance.

When God appeared to Solomon and asked, "What shall I give you?" Solomon asked for wisdom.

In her journal Mother wrote, **"People who desire power always outnumber those who are able to use power wisely once they have it."**

Dear Lord, Thank you for wise leaders who seek your guidance. Give wisdom to those leaders who so badly need it. Amen

2 Chronicles 1:15

Also the king made silver and gold as common in Jerusalem as stones and he made cedars as abundant as the sycamores which are in the lowland.

Solomon was an unusual leader. He used the resources of his country to build a temple for God and enhanced the lives of his people.

Politicians in both parties claim they want to enrich our country, but many citizens suspect they only want to enrich themselves with the power that comes from being elected

There are many good people in positions of authority who try to do the right thing, but if they aren't looking to God for ways to do that, they will only abuse the power they've been given.

In her journal Mother wrote, "Without wisdom and guidance, a person's thirst for power is not satisfied when he gets power. It only becomes more intense (the same thing applies to wealth)".

Dear Lord, Thank you that you have all the power and riches at your disposal. Give us leaders who will turn to You for wisdom. Amen

Deuteronomy 1:12

How can I alone bear your problems and your burdens and your complaints?

Recently one of my daughters said, "Mornings at our house are so hectic that when I finally walk through the door at work, I want to give the signal for **Touch Down**!"

Whether you lead a family, team, organization or a whole nation, being in charge of others is a big responsibility. The only way to do this successfully is to surround yourself with wise people.

God told Moses to delegate some responsibilities to other "wise, understanding and knowledgeable" people in order to reach important goals.

Don't be afraid to ask for help (or too prideful). If you don't let others help, you'll feel overwhelmed and cranky.

In her journal Mother wrote, **"Our goals control our actions. The amount of control is related to the importance of the goal."**

Dear Lord, Thank you for the opportunities you've given us. Help us to give You time each morning so we are the best we can be and send wise, understanding and knowledgeable people to help us reach our destiny. Amen

I Believe She Was a Prophet

This week I read in Deuteronomy that you will know someone is a real prophet if what they predict comes to pass. That reminded me of a visit I had many years ago with two ladies who showed up on my doorstep when we lived in California.

I had a passing acquaintance with one, but I had never seen the other. It was late in the afternoon when they dropped by unannounced, and as I attempted to be a gracious hostess something unusual occurred.

Lydia, the lady I knew, introduced Leigh and explained that they were running some errands and decided to drive through our neighborhood. Our community was situated on an out-of-the-way peninsula so I was surprised.

They came in and as we talked, I noticed Leigh seemed uncomfortable. When our neighbor drove past the window, I commented that he had an interesting job at a record studio and had given the girls some uniquely shaped records.

Leigh said, "That's it! That's why I feel uneasy. The Lord is telling me that there is evil in their family room and you must not let your girls go in their house."

I thought, "Hmm, that's strange," but I checked my spirit and it felt okay so I put my doubt aside I said, "Well actually my husband has already told me that. We've had a few strange encounters and he's not comfortable having them go over there."

Leigh's warning affirmed Don's misgivings.

Months later, our neighbors' children were taken into custody by Children's Services because of abuse. The parents were later indicted on child pornography charges.

During that same visit I mentioned Matt. Leigh again said, "The Lord is telling me that He loves your son and that one day Matt will write a book."

Again, I thought, "Hmmm, that's strange," but I checked my spirit and it felt okay so putting away my doubt I replied, "Probably not because he has some severe developmental issues."

We talked more about Matt before Leigh looked at me and said, "The Lord wants you to know that each night He reaches down and holds Matt close to His heart."

I stopped breathing for a minute. She had just repeated word-for-word my nightly prayers for Matt. Since he began living at the School for the Blind when he was only six until that very day I prayed, *"Lord, please reach down and hold him close since I can't."*

At the time of Leah's visit many unusual and unnerving things were happening in our lives, and I believe she was literally God sent.

When I think of that experience, I realize what a blessing of peace I received, and I continue to pray fervently each night that God will hold Matt close to His heart. I know my prayers are heard, and I don't worry about him.

When I think of my first book, *In My Mother's Words,* and how many of Matt's stories are in it, I realize that in a way he did write a book.

Mother wrote in her journal, **"The Holy Spirit is the one who works to make our prayers acceptable. He enlightens our minds so we may clearly see our desires, then softens our heart so we may feel them and finally He awakens and focuses those desires toward godly things."**

I believe that Leigh was a prophet, and my faith was strengthened by her visit.

Judges 9:53-54

A certain woman dropped a millstone on Abimelech's head and crushed his skull. Then he called to the young man, his armorbearer, and said to him, "Draw you sword and kill me lest men say of me that I was killed by a woman." So the young man thrust him through and he died.

Abimelech thought he was better than anyone else so he had no qualms about killing his brothers and thousands of people who lived in villages he reigned over.

God was displeased and brought Abimelech to a tower in a town called Thebez.

Abimelech meant to burn the tower with the town's people in it as he had done before, but one woman (maybe a miller's wife or daughter) threw her millstone from the top of the tower and cracked his skull.

He lived in pride and he died thinking he was too good to be killed by a woman.

Mother wrote in her journal, **"Abimelech was fatally wounded by a woman."** That's all she had to say about him.

Dear Lord, defeat the spirit of pride in my life. It is evil and I rebuke it in Jesus name. Amen

1 Samuel 13:30

Then Samuel said to Saul, "You have done foolishly. You have not kept the commandment of the Lord your God, which He commanded you. For now the Lord would have established your kingdom over Israel forever."

God chose Saul to be the first king of Israel and for a while he did a great job. When Saul assumed he knew what to do in his own wisdom, his life began to unravel, and he opened the door for other sins to enter his heart.

There is nothing sadder than watching a godly person making choices that take him/her away from God.

In her journal Mother wrote, **"No matter how much good we do for God's kingdom, sin in our lives will still produce powerful and damaging consequences."**

Dear Father, Thank you for planning good things for us. Help us to keep you always first in our hearts. Show us our mistakes, and make us repentant when we turn away from your will. Amen

Deuteronomy 1:13

Choose wise and understanding men from among your tribes and I will make them heads over you.

Mark Twain commented, "An honest person in politics shines more there than he/she would elsewhere."

It seems to me that the only way to lead successfully is to get up early, read the Bible and pray for wisdom and strength for the day. Everything is doable after that.

Everybody is susceptible to the heady aroma of authority so to avoid the pitfalls of corruption God says we should surround ourselves with wise people who understand what's really going on. Leaders who surround themselves with "yes men" rarely see the real picture.

In her journal Mother wrote, **"So much unnecessary suffering takes place because we don't call on God until we have used up all other resources. Rather than waiting until the situation becomes desperate, turn to God first. He has the necessary resources to meet every kind of problem.**

Dear Father, Thank you for your Son, Jesus who saves us and for the Holy Spirit who reveals Truth. Give us leaders who call on You. Amen

Deuteronomy 1:21

Look, the Lord your God has set the land before you. Go up and possess it as the Lord God of your fathers has spoken to you; do not fear or be discouraged.

Before ever taking the field for any football game, a good coach makes a game plan. He knows his players strengths and the opponent's weaknesses.

God has a plan for our lives and even thought we don't always know what the future holds, we can be confident that He has it under control. We can be bold and unafraid knowing the lives He has prepared for us.

Faith in Christ gives us boldness and helps us overcome defeats and discouragements because we believe God has planned good things for us.

Mother wrote in her journal, **"God prepares you for the future."**

Dear Lord, Thank you for the plans you have for us. Show us the way you would have us go and make us fearless.

Deuteronomy 1: 36

Caleb shall see it (the Promised Land) and to him and his children I am giving the land on which he walked because he wholly followed the Lord.

God trusted him with the task of scouting out the Promised Land and its inhabitants.

Being trustworthy, he did exactly what was required of him, but when he returned with his report, the people became afraid at the thought of taking the land from inhabitants who were physical giants.

God held Caleb accountable for his actions not their reactions.

In her journal Mother wrote, **"God does not want promises for the future but obedience for the day. We need to be careful to place our trust only in people who are trustworthy."**

Dear Lord, Help us to seek your will and follow your commands. Thank you that we can trust You in all things. Amen

Deuteronomy 1:38

But Joshua, the son of Nun, who stands before you, he shall go in there (the Promised Land). Encourage him for he shall cause Israel to inherit it.

One of my favorite coaches is Tony Dungy. He is an encourager.

"Things will go wrong at times. You can't always control circumstances. However, you can always control your attitude, approach and response. Your options are to complain or look ahead and figure out how to make the situation better.

Be ready to encourage others in leadership positions and lead when it is your turn to lead, but only if you can take the responsibility of leadership decisions.

In her journal Mother wrote, **"The measure of your trustworthiness is your willingness to take responsibility for what you say or do, even if you must pay a painful price."**

Dear Lord, Thank you for the encouragement we can find in Your Word. Help us take responsibility for our all our decisions. Amen

Deuteronomy 2: 30

But the Lord your God hardened his (King Sihon) spirit and made his heart obstinate that God might deliver him into your hand as it is this day.

Sometimes you're going along saying your prayers and minding your own business and an unexpected situation pops up. There is conflict and suddenly you have an opponent.

Don't worry. God has sent you here or allowed you to be in this place for a reason. There are no victories without adversaries.

In her journal Mother wrote, **"Unbelievers will not listen to what we say unless we back it up with the way we live."**

Dear Lord, Give me wisdom to overcome the obstacles and adversaries you place in my life, and let me do so in a way that will glorify Your name. Amen

Deuteronomy 3:22

You must not fear them for the Lord your God Himself fights for you.

The greatest adversary is also the greatest liar who says you are not good enough. He belittles your accomplishments and throws your failures in your face.

Don't listen! Because of Christ's sacrifice on the cross, you are righteous and extraordinary in his sight. He has a special plan for your life. Claim Christ who fights for you.

In her journal Mother wrote, **"The Lord takes ordinary things and people and does extraordinary things."**

Dear Lord, You ways are infinitely higher than I can imagine. Thank you for always having my back in every situation. Deliver us from the evil one. Amen

Joel 2:25

I will restore to you the years that the swarming locust have eaten.

Few of us can look back over our lives and not have some regrets. We wonder, "What if," but continually doubting our choices is one of the enemy's most successful weapons.

When I visit a relative who lives in a nursing home, one of the things he says most often is, "I should have." Although he was talented in many areas, poor health and misfortune dominated his life and left him with regrets.

After a recent visit, I thanked the activity director for one of the many nice things she does for my relative. She smiled and said, "He blesses us every day."

Mother wrote in her journal, **"It is sad to be remembered for what might have been, but it is never too late to start over. However badly we have failed in the past, today is not too late for us to put our complete trust in Him."**

Father, I thank you for never giving up on us. Deflect the enemy's darts of doubt with the knowledge of your eternal love. Amen

Study the Word and You Will Know The Truth

A movie starring Russell Crowe, a Bible study by Lisa Harper and a women's conference featuring Carole Avriett all combined to increase my joy in the Lord.

My Bible study is on Hebrews and it was written by Lisa Harper. She is a Bible scholar who uses stories and humor to draw me in. Each week she provides at least one "Aha" moment for me.

What I take away from these studies enhances my spiritual growth and though I've been reading and studying The Word all of my adult life, I find there is still so much to learn. That's a joy and I look forward to the weekly preparations.

I signed up for a recent women's conference and was blessed by the featured speaker, Carole Avriett, whose publishing and speaking career spans over twenty-five years. When Carole enters a room she brings grace and knowledge with her.

She spent fourteen years as Home Editor for *Southern Living Magazine* producing hundreds of articles on architecture and interior design. She also co-edited <u>At Home With Southern Living.</u> This lady has style and the creds to go with it.

Her teaching is covered in prayer and bolstered by her research. Her sessions were full of wisdom and a love for the Lord that gave me joy.

Now to Russell Crowe, last week we went to see the movie that so many people talked about, *Noah*.

"It's a Bible story," I reasoned. "Promoting entertainment from The Word has got to be a good thing." So off we went to the movie theater where we purchased our tickets, popcorn, drinks, and took our seats in the nearly empty area for the matinee showing.

From the first note of the musical score that accompanied the written prologue to the fallen angels who were portrayed as a cross between Transformers and gray Incredible Hulks, we prepared to watch a fantasy. The whole movie was a clever mix of Noah's soul searching and fantastic special effects which could easily lead some to reason that since this movie, based on a Bible story, was fantasy then the Bible itself is fiction.

Though that idea made me sad, my joy came from knowing the Word personally and I was not deceived. If you know the difference between fiction and nonfiction (Truth), you can read and enjoy both. Knowing the Word is essential to our faith.

In her journal Mother wrote, "**When the Holy Spirit works there is movement, excitement and growth. He gives us motivation, energy and ability to get the gospel to the whole world.**"

Knowing His Word reveals His Truth in everything -even a fantastical movie about a major Bible character.

Job 32:9

Great men are not always wise, nor do the aged always understand justice.

A few years ago, a man ran for president. He was successful in his profession. His wife of many years was also successful and together they had four children. They had weathered a major tragedy and held to each other and their faith.

As a family they waded into the national political arena and their combined efforts were paying off until he chose to have an affair with a staff member.

Well, the rest is history. Before he had a chance to watch with supporters as his results came in on election night, he instead watched as his life unraveled in front of the whole world. It was a sad situation made sadder because it was so public.

In her journal Mother wrote, **"Great strength in one area of life does not make up for great weaknesses in other areas."**

Dear Lord, You told us that all of us have sinned and fall short of your glory. Help us, Lord, to seek your strength daily because it delights the enemy when we fail. Amen

Deuteronomy 3:28

But command Joshua and encourage him and strengthen him for he shall go over before his people and he shall cause them to inherit the land which you will see.

Moses' temper cost him the opportunity to lead his people into the Promised Land himself, but God gave him another great task. He was to command, strengthen and encourage the next leader - Joshua.

Parents, pastors, coaches and teachers are allowed the privilege of mentoring young people. It is a role that can make a tremendous difference in their lives and the kingdom of heaven.

The strongest people I know are the ones, who in spite of their failures had someone encourage them to try again.

In her journal Mother wrote, **"God can use a person of faith in spite of his/her mistakes."**

Dear Lord, Thank you for mentors. Protect them and use them for Your glory in the lives of young people. Amen

Deuteronomy 4: 41-42

Then Moses set aside three cities. . that the manslayer might flee there, who kills his neighbor unintentionally without having hated him in time past and that by fleeing to these cities he might live.

There is a popular TV show titled <u>Revenge</u>. The plot is a weekly cycle of payback dispatched, by the lovely heroine, to those responsible for wronging her father. I watched for a few episodes but could see no upside for anyone.

A heart full of blame is heavy baggage to lug around and makes the one carrying it a victim.

Mother wrote in her journal, **"Revenge is an uncontrollable monster. Each act of retaliation brings another. It is a boomerang that cannot be thrown without cost to the thrower. The revenge cycle can be halted only by forgiveness."**

Dear Lord, My sins are so many, but I flee to You for forgiveness and refuge. Help me to have a forgiving heart. Amen

Deuteronomy 3:26

But the Lord was angry with me on your account and would not listen to me.

Moses lost his temper and his anger lost him the opportunity to enter the Promised Land.

A young man showed potential as a running back until he suffered a severe knee injury. He worked hard in rehab and returned to practice the next spring only to injure it again.

The disappointment made him angry and anger caused him feel separated from God which was just what Satan wanted.

God can handle our anger and wait for us to return.

In her journal Mother wrote, **"One of the effects of sin in our life is to keep us from wanting to pray. Don't let guilty feelings over sin keep you from your only means of restoration. No matter how long you have been away from God, He is ready to hear from you and restore you to a right relationship."**

Dear Lord, Thank you for those who pray for us when we can't or won't come to you. Deliver us from evil so our guilt won't separate us from you. Amen

Deuteronomy 4:5

"Surely I have taught you statutes and judgments, just as the Lord my God commanded me that you should act according to them in the land which you go to possess.

Life is chaotic without some type of discipline that usually consists of rules, consequences and rewards. The rules are reasonable, the consequences for choosing not to follow them are unpleasant and the rewards for choosing to follow the rules are something we desire.

We learn to make wise choices and receive rewards, but there are some people who are genuinely obedient without expectation of reward. They see the need for rules and choose to follow them.

In her journal Mother wrote, **"Selfish obedience does not bring us far. Genuine obedience is motivated by a love and reverence for God himself."**

Dear Lord, Thank you for going all the way to the cross without thought of consequences or rewards. Your only motivation was love. Help our lives reflect our love for You. Amen

Proverbs 5:21

The ways of man are before the eyes of the Lord, and He ponders all his paths.

My mother was ahead of her time in many ways. One was her instruction to me on my behavior when she wasn't around. She told me that according to the Bible, God saw and heard everything. It was a spiritual concept and overrode any major fear when the Big Brother theory of government came up later in my life.

Of course I did things I shouldn't have done, but I probably did less of them because of what she told me. We in turn gave our daughters the same instruction.

With smart phones and social media, it is a wise person who behaves because a loving God is watching.

In her journal Mother wrote, **"To know what is really right and have the strength to do it, we need to draw closer to God and His word."**

Dear Lord, Thank you for parents who know your word and teach it to their children. Help us to remember that You listen and watch because you love us. Amen

1 Samuel 3:9

Therefore Eli said to Samuel, "Go lie down; and it shall be, if He calls you, that you must say, 'Speak, Lord, for Your servant hears.'" So Samuel went and lay down in his place.

Eli raised Samuel to recognize God's voice and follow His instructions. Eli must have been a good teacher because Samuel grew, and when God spoke Samuel listened and obeyed.

Samuel became a prophet and a judge. When the people demanded a king, Samuel listened to God and anointed Saul.

Eli's guidance helped Samuel accomplish great things and standout in history as a man of honor.

Mother wrote in her journal, **"A person's greatest accomplishment may well be helping others accomplish great things. Likewise, a person's greatest failure may be preventing others from achieving greatness."**

Dear Lord, Thank you for those who give us wise instruction. Help us to seek Your wisdom and pass it on to the next generation. Amen

Esther 4:16

"Go gather all the Jews who are present in Shushan and fast for me; neither eat nor drink for three days, night or day. My maids and I will fast likewise, and so I will go to the king, which is against the law, and if I perish, I perish."

Esther had an opportunity to do something great, but if she failed the consequences were dire. She prepared herself through fasting. Her preparation paid off because she found the courage to go to the king. She found favor in his sight and he asked what she wanted.

Several years ago a godly lady suggested a couple with a special needs child fast and pray for their son's future. It seemed, at the time, a strange suggestion, but we did it.

Within the year their special son settled into a wonderful situation where he could live for his lifetime on earth and since they are confident of where he will spend eternity – his future is secure.

In her journal Mother wrote, **"Godliness cannot be merely a claim. It must be a reality in our motives and in our actions."**

Dear Father, Nudge our spirits into fasting and prayer so we may have strength and wisdom to act when you ask us to. Amen

Deuteronomy 4:14

And the Lord commanded me at that time to teach you statutes and judgments that you might observe them in the land you cross over to possess (The Promised Land).

Each of us has a journey to The Promised Land. It's called Life and God intends for us to boldly claim our futures. He gives us judgments and statutes (rules and regulations) that prepare us for success, but without Him we won't attain the lives He has planned for us.

Mother wrote in her journal, **"When you leave God out of your life, you may be shocked at what you are capable of doing. We will lose the battle if we gather the spoils of earthly treasure rather than seeking the treasure of heaven."**

Dear Lord, Help us to attain the Promised Land you have planned for us. Bind Satan in any attempt he would make to lead us away from You. Amen

Deuteronomy 4:39

Therefore, know this day and consider it in your heart that the Lord Himself is God in heaven above and on earth beneath; there is no other.

According to the U. S. State Department, an American pastor was recently sentenced to eight years in prison for preaching the gospel in a country where this is considered blasphemy.

A spokesman for the department called on Iran to respect his human rights and release him, but he remains imprisoned.

He may be the only Christian other inmates and prison guards ever see and like the Apostle Paul have the opportunity to glorify "the Lord Himself of heaven above and earth beneath".

Mother wrote in her journal, "**Even in times of crisis and deepest despair, there are those who follow God and through whom God works.**"

Dear Lord, give us strength and power through your Holy Spirit to witness for you. We ask a special working of your Spirit for the Christians who are held in prison only because they love you. Amen

Be An Overcomer

Last weekend I attended a *Champion Within* luncheon sponsored by the Tennessee Sports Hall of Fame honoring champions who have overcome substantial obstacles to achieve success in athletics. They are champions despite disabilities.

The *Champion Within* youth program is designed to encourage young people to rise above obstacles in life and to believe in themselves.

A room full of people watched as each athlete took the stage, received the award, and gave a short acceptance speech.

Rashard Witherspoon, a junior at the Tennessee School for the Deaf High School, made a name for himself as a hardworking athlete. In football, he was named All American by the Deaf Digest and NDIAA for 2012 &2013. In basketball he was placed on the All Viking Classic team and made All- Tournament and All District teams.

Rashard is also competing with other deaf students across the country in a national CrossFit challenge, works on computers and loves to spend time with his family.

This young man says he knows that with God all things are possible and with humility he thanked God and his family for helping him achieve so much.

Joshua Putman was also honored. Joshua was born with Down's syndrome and early on his parents enrolled him in programs that helped him stay active and healthy. He began competing in Special Olympics at eight years old and still competes.

Josh participated on his high school wrestling team and won gold medals in swimming, flag football, basketball, power lifting, track and field, volleyball, snowboarding, bowling and golf. He, of course, hit a hole in one.

In 1998 Josh was selected as the Tennessee Special Olympics Athlete of the Year. Soon Josh will compete with his partner, Steve Overlock, in the 2014 USA Games in Unified Golf.

Josh's strong will, great attitude and supportive family drives him to work hard, and his hard work enables him to overcome adversity. He helps others by volunteering and participating in the annual Polar Plunge.

After Josh proudly received his award he thanked his parents, coaches and others who had helped him, and then with a catch in his throat he declared, "I really am a champion!"

During the standing ovation,, I saw several tears quickly wiped away as we were reminded that champions aren't just gifted athletes. They are overcomers who won't be stopped by adversity.

We have our own champion in the family, our son Matt. He was born with serious and multiple problems that will require special care all his life but against all odds, he thrives. Watching his daily battles and hearing stories of how other people with disabilities have achieved success gives me little patience for folks who are blessed with strong minds and bodies yet won't even try.

A quote by Booker T. Washington says it all, "Success is to be measured not so much by the position that one has reached in life as by the obstacles which he has overcome while trying to succeed."

Mother wrote in her journal, **"God will not hold us accountable for gifts he has not given us, but all of us are responsible to use fully the gifts we do have."**

Deuteronomy 5:1

And Moses called all Israel and said to them, "Hear O Israel, the statutes and judgments which I speak in your hearing today, that you may learn them and be careful to observe them."

When the kids were little we lived in a college town where we made many friends. One young lady, Gail, was a student from New England. She would spend hours at our home. Our backgrounds were different as were our ages, but conversation came easily and though Gail wasn't a believer, she was open to our life style and our faith.

Eventually she asked to know more about the Lord. It was a joy to tell her and hear her accept Jesus as her Savior.

Christians follow statutes and judgments set down in scripture, but more importantly we follow a Savior, Jesus Christ who gives us a hope that fills us with peace and joy no matter what life is dishing up. When that happens those who know us want to know Him.

In her journal Mother wrote, **"Sharing openly about our relationship with God can bring depth and intimacy to our relationship with others."**

Dear Lord, Thank you for your word which gives us a standard for living. Thank you for Christ who is our Savior. Help us live our faith in Him. Amen

Deuteronomy 5:7

Thou shalt have no other God before Me.

My grandchildren are avid sports fans and Tim Tebow is one of their favorite players. He isn't the favorite because he set records at Florida or won the Heisman Trophy. They admire him because he lives Deuteronomy 5:7 in front of millions.

He was often ridiculed and mocked for *Tbowing* after touchdowns and giving God the glory for his success. His NFL career was short, but God had something better and Tim Tebow trusted Him as he waited.

In her journal Mother wrote, **"Your reputation is formed by the people who watch you at work, in town, at home, in church. A good reputation comes by consistently living out the qualities you believe in no matter what group of people or surroundings you are in. A person's actions reflect his/her character."**

Dear Lord, Thank you for your word that tells us how to behave. Help us to live lives that glorify You. Amen

Deuteronomy 29:29

The secret things belong to the Lord our God, but those things which are revealed belong to us and to our children forever, that we may do all the words of the law.

As I read this I remembered a conversation I had with a teenage grandson, "Meme, lots of my friends don't believe the Bible is true." Their unbelief concerned him.

We talked awhile and I thought of today's scripture. I didn't quote him chapter and verse, but I did say, "You know, God's thoughts and ways are so much bigger than ours that there is no way we would understand it all if He told us everything. He gives us what we can handle and He gives it through His Word. We are expected to believe it."

In her journal Mother wrote, **"Events do not occur by luck or coincidence. We should have faith that God is directing our lives for His purpose."**

Dear Father, Thank you for directing our lives for your purpose. Give us faith to believe the secrets you reveal in your word. Amen

Deuteronomy 5:11

You shall not take the name of the Lord your God in vain for the Lord will not hold him guiltless who takes His name in vain.

One of my favorite TV characters is a Navy Seal. He plays the part of a hero, but he is not the real deal. He is only pretending. When he leaves the set he can't continue his ruse.

Deuteronomy 5:11 tells us not to pretend to be what we aren't. When we profess our faith in Christ we make a serious commitment to God. True believers are people of character who have the hearts and minds of God. We no longer belong to ourselves – we belong to Him.

In her journal Mother wrote, **"Heroes simply do the right thing at the right time. They tend to think of others before they think of themselves."**

Dear Lord, Thank you for true believers who put You first, others second and themselves last. Help us to live a life true to You.

Ruth 3:1

Then Naomi her mother-in-law said to her, "My daughter, shall I not seek security for you, so that it may be well with you"

After returning from WWII, my dad married Mother and enrolled at a state college on the GI bill. When I came along, he decided it was more important to work and support his family so he dropped out of college.

He regretted not finishing his degree, and often told his story to encourage and motivate us to get our degrees.

In her journal Mother wrote, **"Each of us knows a parent or older friend or relative who is always looking out for our best interest. Be willing to listen to the advice of those who are older and wiser than you are.**

Dear Lord, Thank you for the wise council of those older and wiser than we are. Help us to repay that wisdom with kindness and respect. Amen

Joshua 3:7

And the Lord said to Joshua, "This day I will begin to magnify you in the sight of all Israel, that they may know that, as I was with Moses, so I will be with you".

Joshua was the new leader and he had a mission to accomplish. He was to lead the Israelites into the Promised Land. Because Joshua successfully followed God's plan, the people knew God was with Joshua just as He had been with Moses.

Before we follow any one, we must have faith in that person and trust what he/she says. God always does what He says He will do, and we can trust him because, as David Livingston said, "It is the word of a gentleman of the most strict and sacred honor, so there's an end of it!"

In her journal Mother wrote, **"Keeping your word and following through on assignments should be high on anyone's priority list. Building a reputation for integrity, however, must be done one brick, one act at a time."**

Dear Lord, thank you for always keeping your word to us. Help us to be people of integrity so we reflect your nature in our lives and draw others to you. Amen

Isaiah 30:25

There will be on every high mountain and on every high hill rivers and streams of waters. In the day of the great slaughter when the towers fall.

Every time I read this scripture, I think of 9/11/2001. I was teaching third grade and had walked my class to the computer lab where the lab teacher whispered, "We've been attacked."

The rest of the day was spent trying to find out as much information as possible without alarming the students.

Instant media and 24/7 news make us witnesses to "great slaughter", but we also hear follow up stories of heroes who become "rivers and streams of waters".

In her journal Mother wrote, **"Even in our sorrow and calamity, God can bring great blessings. Trust God. He will be with you in the hard times."**

Dear Lord, Thank you for the times you have delivered us from evil. Give us eyes to see what we need to see and courage knowing that you are always with us. Amen

Deuteronomy 5:12

Observe the Sabbath day to keep it holy.

We live in a 24/7 world. News, entertainment or work can be accessed anytime. It seems very caring of God to command that we take a day off to enjoy family and friends. The secret is in seeking a holy perspective apart from that of a rowdy world.

God has important work for us and we can be most effective when we are rested and focused on Him. Work hard six days a week but rest on the Sabbath.

Mother wrote in her journal, **"We will not know the full purpose and importance of our lives until we are able to look back on the perspective of eternity."**

Dear Lord, Thank you for giving us a day to rest so we can be our best. Amen

Deuteronomy 5:16

Honor your father and mother . . .that your days may be long and that it may be well with you in the land which the Lord your God is giving you.

My memories of my grandfather were so sweet it surprised me to learn that for much of his life my Papa was an alcoholic. He quit after hearing a sermon at a summer revival when he was in his fifties.

His children treated him with love and respect even though his behavior often embarrassed and hurt them. From them I learned how to extend forgiveness and to pray for those I love.

If you don't have perfect parents, love them and respect them anyway. If God commands it that means there is a reason, and you will be a witness to them.

In her journal Mother wrote, **Live in faithfulness to God, knowing that the significance of your life will extend beyond your lifetime. The rewards will outweigh any sacrifice you may have made."**

Dear Lord, Thank you for our parents. Help us to honor them as You commanded. Amen

Deuteronomy 5:16, 17, 18, 19

You shall not murder. You shall not commit adultery. You shall not steal. You shall not bear false witness against your neighbor.

Every game I know of has rules. In the game of Life, the goal is to attain your Promised Land – the life God has planned for you, and He has provided some rules.

He tells us over and over in His Word to be bold as you play this game, but in your boldness you must also develop the character and spirit He wants for you.

If you play the game of Life without lying, cheating or stealing then there are no regrets when you reach the goal.

In her journal Mother wrote, **"Determine to run your race as God's person from start to finish."**

Dear Lord, Give us boldness to reach our Promised Land. Help us play by Your rules. Amen

Trust His Word

Today a friend shared this snippet from a Rick Warren devotional, "Life can be tough, and we all get discouraged. The fact is you are never going to be an effective Christian if you try to go it alone. You need other people. Snowflakes are frail, but if enough of them stick together they can stop traffic."

My Sunday school class is full of snowflakes. Yesterday our lesson from Ecclesiastes reminded us that life will have sorrow as well as joy. Solomon in his wisdom says to enjoy the good times and learn from the sorrow.

As Sunday's lesson came to an end we had a time of discussion and that's when the snowflakes joined together and shared their strength.

Two sweet ladies told of their experiences caring for elderly parents. There were the widows who learned that God provides in their new singleness. There are those who, because of their spouses' Alzheimer's disease, are single.

All their testimonies touched my heart, but one especially resonated. It came from a lady who always has a smile and a spiffy look so I assumed she had a super-duper life.

She said, "When my husband began to lose his mind, I thought it couldn't get any worse. Then stress caused me to have a break down, and I thought it couldn't get any worse.

While I was having my personal pity party, a dear friend lost her young son and I realized it can always get worse."

When God brought us to faith, He knew we would be tested, and He provided promises to claim during those times.

In her journal Mother wrote, **"Even if life is difficult now, one day we will rejoice. We must keep our eyes on the future and on God's promises."**

Whatever you're going through, God provides a promise in His word that will speak to your heart and help you get through it. Just like the ladies in my Sunday school class.

Deuteronomy 5:21

You shall not covet your neighbor's wife or his house, his field his manservant or his maidservant or anything that is your neighbors.

When you covet you're jealous of what someone else has. Coveting takes your joy, contentment, relationships and in extreme cases lives.

My friend has a small house, no children or significant other yet she is one of the happiest people I know. She is perfectly content because she doesn't compare her life to anyone else's.

The saddest, meanest, angriest people I know are those who want what belongs to another, and as they focus on what others possess they lose sight of their own blessings

Mother wrote in her journal, **"God has special rewards for His people, but not everyone will receive them in this life".**

Dear Lord, Thank you for all the blessings you have given me. I claim them in joy and thankfulness. Take away any coveting and jealousy living in my heart. Amen

Isaiah 40:31

Those who wait on the Lord shall renew their strength. They shall mount up with wings like eagles. They shall run and not be weary. They shall walk and not faint.

When I look back over my life, I see how every new opportunity was preceded by a time of waiting.

During the waiting period we anticipated what would be next; wondered, imagined and sometimes worried about what the future held, and when the next thing came, we were renewed and ready for another challenge.

Be patient while God prepares the next chapter in your life.

Mother wrote in her journal, **"The difficult circumstances in life and the times of waiting often refine, teach, and prepare us for the future opportunities God has for us."**

Dear Lord, Thank you for periods of waiting and renewing. Bless those who today feel reined in by their circumstances. Help them to take this time as a blessing to ready them for the future. Amen

Psalm 103:1-2

Bless the Lord, O my soul and all that is within me, bless His holy name. Bless the Lord, O my soul and forget not all His benefits.

We were living in Kansas and spring was taking its time arriving to melt the eight inches of snow on the ground. The bright sun lit the azure sky over trees that would wear their white diamond cloaks for a while longer.

The country road to my school wound to the left, and in the curve three startled deer lifted their heads and looked at me. Without thinking, I waved, smiled and half expected them to return my greeting.

The drive that winter morning reminded me of His many benefits and blessings.

In her journal Mother wrote, **"God desires that all our work and worship be motivated by genuine heart felt devotion to Him.**

Dear Lord, You are so worthy of praise and the praise pleases you and renews us. Thank you Father. Amen

Deuteronomy 6:5

You shall love the Lord your God with all your heart, with all your soul and all your mind.

Today, I am thankful for my fellow Christians. Each one is a cell in the body of Christ that brings light to a dark world.

I'm thankful for the thousands of missionaries who felt the Holy Spirit's call and left the comforts of home and loved ones to carry the gospel far and wide; and for the people who gave financial and moral support for this cause.

I'm thankful for pastors and worship leaders who speak truth to their congregations, and for Christian parents who make living the gospel in front of their children a constant priority.

Those who love the Lord with all their hearts, souls and minds please Him and inspire others to dedicate their lives to Him.

In her journal Mother wrote, **"God's faithfulness and love should inspire us to dedicate our lives to Him completely. We must never take His mercy for granted."**

Dear Lord, Thank you for Christian brothers and sisters everywhere. Bless and protect them so they may continue to glorify Your name Amen

Deuteronomy 6:6-7

And these words shall be in your heart and you shall teach them to your children and talk of them when you sit in your house, when you walk by the way; when you lie down and when you rise up.

Growing up, most of my school friends also attended church with me. Through the years I made many other friends, but I feel closest to the ones who learned John 3:16 when I did.

Growing up, we dealt with major events that brought us to our knees, and we trusted Him to bring us through our darkest times.

We were blessed with parents, teachers and coaches who took Deuteronomy 6:6-7 to heart and in doing so pointed us to Christ.

Mother wrote in her journal, **"All we have and receive is on loan from God. Teach that to your children."**

Heavenly Father, Thank you for people who live lives true to what You teach. Amen

Deuteronomy 7:13

And He will love and bless you and multiply you. He will also bless the fruit of your womb and the fruit of your land. . .

When I was eight, I came home from a summer revival, put on my pajamas, climbed into bed and was suddenly overwhelmed by my sinfulness.

Mother came to tuck me in and understood what was happening. We talked, prayed and I asked Jesus into my heart that night.

Many years later my daughters had similar experiences and when they became mothers they saw their children come to know Him.

In her journal Mother wrote, **"The greatest story ever told is the story of Jesus taking our sins on Himself, dying on the cross and defeating death when he rose again."**

Dear Lord, Thank You for Your mercy, grace and salvation. Help us to lead lives that draw others to You. Amen

Deuteronomy 8:5

So you should know in your heart as a man (parent) chastens his son (child) so the Lord your God chastens you.

No child likes to be disciplined, but most children need to know there will be a consequence for unacceptable behavior. Providing appropriate discipline is in every parent's job description.

Recently I read a book by an award winning author who has made millions writing about the harsh discipline doled out to him and his siblings by an abusive father. In the author's memory, there was nothing positive about his father's approach or relationship to his children yet they are all successful.

This caused me to wonder if the childhood recollections of the author are as valid as his best-selling book suggests. It certainly made for good reading.

One thing Christians can count on: God's discipline will always be appropriate for making us who He wants us to be.

In her journal Mother wrote, "**Being a parent involves a life time of hard work, consistent expectations and making difficult decisions.**"

Dear Lord, I don't like to be disciplined, but I receive it knowing it keeps me in Your will. Amen

Deuteronomy 11:26-28

Behold, I set before you today a blessing and a curse. The blessing if you obey the commandments; and the curse if you do not obey the commandments of the Lord your God.

After watching hundreds of ballgames, I can truthfully say every player was expected to follow a set of carefully thought out rules. In sports, disobeying a rule is called a foul and the team who has the fewest fouls usually wins.

Our wise God has provided rules which we call commandments, and if we obey them we are more likely to make wise choices that lead to blessings rather than poor choices which lead to regrets.

In her journal Mother wrote, **"Learning His way and listening is vital in our relationship with Him. We must listen and then act upon what He tells us."**

Dear Lord, thank you for providing us with rules for life. Help us to follow those rules so we may be blessed. Amen

Deuteronomy 15: 11

For the poor will never cease from the land, therefore I command you saying, "You shall open your hand wide to your brother, to your poor and your needy in your land."

Anyone who has struggled financially and received a kindness can appreciate this verse. God doesn't just ask us to help the poor, He demands it.

My parents made a bedroom available in their small house when a widow needed special attention. My mother-in-law regularly cooked enough food for her family and a nearby family of eight.

When we help others, it is pleasing to Him and blesses us.

My mother wrote in her journal, **"When you serve others – even in carrying out ordinary tasks – you are serving God. Because ultimately we serve God, every job has dignity.**

Dear Lord, Thank you for opportunities to open our hands and hearts to others. Help us remember every task is for You and Your glory. Amen

Isaiah 45:9

Woe to him who strives with his Maker! Let the potsherd strive with the potsherds of the earth. Shall the clay say to him who forms it, "What are you making?"

God doesn't have the same purpose in mind for all of us. The fact is that not all of us are going to be superstars. Not all of us are going to be missionaries or great men like Moses, Daniel, Peter and Paul. Some of us are just made for common use.

If God wants to use you for a special purpose then the turning of The Potter's wheel will be greater in your life than in those around you, and you will feel the pressure. If this applies to your current circumstance, trust that He is making you a special vessel for His glory.

Mother wrote in her journal, **"God uses His power according to His own wisdom and will. He responds to the faith of those who seek Him."**

Dear Lord, Thank you for the special use you have for each of us. Forgive us for doubting when we face the pressure that turns us into vessels that best serve You. Amen

Spring

Blue skies, early blossoms and singing birds – it's a spring thing! Yesterday was officially the first day of that renewing season, and I'm hoping Some One told the weather to cooperate.

More cold temperatures could still be in store for us, there have been snowfalls during a few spring breaks, but for all practical purposes the end of winter is here.

In an effort to chase away the winter blues, last week I got out the Easter bunnies and placed them strategically around the house, but I made myself wait until spring's official beginning to hang the carrot wreath on the front door.

The rabbits and carrots make me think of Easter – the observance of Christ's death and resurrection. This celebration of faith is both the saddest of times yet the most joyful. The forty days before Easter provide a time of introspection and a tiny insight into sacrifice.

C. S. Lewis is one of my favorite authors and I love his quote, "Easter is chocolate eggs and Christ risen". What could be any better than that?

Usually I stroll the candy aisle of our local grocery store and fill my basket with chocolate eggs and bunnies, but this year we gave up chocolate for Lent.

Everywhere I turn there seems to be an overflowing of chocolate confectionaries, and as I gaze longingly at the rich treat I remind myself that it's a no-no. The only good my self-imposed restriction serves is to give me a minute glimpse of sacrifice.

Spring is the result of sacrifice. The seeds that were buried last fall will rise up through the ground and provide beans and corn and grains to feed us.

The forsythia that lost its leaves and stood bare through this icy winter wakes up and pops with yellow blooms.

Drowsy animals awaken hungry for life and those of us who have experienced the winter blues and loss of joy will feel the sun's warmth revive our spirits.

This quote by Vance Havner, a powerful pastor from the Carolinas, sums it up, *"God uses broken things. It takes broken soil to produce a crop, broken clouds to give rain, broken grain to give bread, broken bread to give strength. It is the broken alabaster box that gives forth perfume. It is Peter, weeping bitterly who returns to greater power than ever."*

Spring is wonderful in its ability to renew brokenness not only in the earth but also in us.

Mother wrote in her journal, **"Spring is wonderful in its ability to renew brokenness not only in the earth but also in us. Even if life is difficult now, one day we will rejoice. Keep your eyes on the future and on God's promises."**

Joshua 1:9

Have I not commanded you, "Be of good courage; do not be afraid nor be dismayed for the Lord your God is with you wherever you go?"

As a child I memorized this scripture, but the verse took on a special meaning for me when our son was born with severe multiple handicaps. I have claimed this promise on many occasions since that diagnosis over forty years ago.

Our church recently finished a series of messages on Grace and the congregation watched videos of members sharing their grace experiences during difficult times. Faced with terrible difficulties, these stories reflected the hope found because of the grace of God.

In her journal Mother wrote, **"Even in our sorrow and calamity, God can bring great blessings. Trust God. He will be with you in the hard times."**

Dear Lord, Thank you for grace that gives us strength to endure. Please be with those who are today wondering if they can make it. Help them be of good courage, and know You are always with them. Amen

Joshua 3:5

And Joshua said to the people, "Sanctify yourselves for tomorrow the Lord will do wonders among you."

Joshua was a courageous young man who witnessed God's miracles. Believing God had more wonders in store, Joshua encouraged his people to be sanctified (live according to God's purpose).

During different periods (places) in our lives we absolutely saw the hand of God at work. I remember those times with wonder, but today's scripture says we will see more wondrous things if we will believe and live to please Him.

In her journal Mother wrote, **"People often try to live on the memories of God's blessing, but His mercies are new every day."**

Dear Lord, Thank you for all you have done for me in the past, and stir my spirit to a relationship with You that is also present tense. Amen

Joshua 23:3

"You have seen all that the Lord your God has done to all these nations because of you, for the Lord your God is He who has fought for you."

We may be "grandfathered" into some benefits, but a relationship with God isn't one of them. Each person must choose whom he/she will serve, and if Jesus Christ is the choice we want to spend time with Him every day.

We are blessed to live in a country made free by the faith and sacrifices of generations before us, and I believe His people will continue to be blessed as long as we remember our strength comes from God.

Mother wrote in her journal, **"Today, as in Bible times, spiritual victories come through continually renewing your relationship with Him. Keep your relationship new and fresh."**

Dear Lord, Thank you for loving us. Help us to seek you each day for guidance and strength. Amen

Kings 1:5-6

Now Adonijah, the son of Haggith, exalted himself . . . .and his father (King David) had not rebuked him at any time . . .

This handsome young man lived in a palace where, according to this verse, he could pretty much do as he pleased.

Without discipline his pride grew and he decided he should be king. After his failed attempt to take the throne from his brother Solomon, Solomon forgave him and said, "Go to your house."

He could have had a rich, rewarding life, but his pride lead him to feel entitled to special privileges he hadn't earned. He eventually hatched another plot asking for Abishag, a young woman very close to King David., and Solomon interpreted the request as another attempt to usurp the throne. That was the end of Adonijah.

In her journal Mother wrote, **"When sin dominates our lives, even God-given joys and pleasures seem empty."**

Dear Lord, Thank you for disciplining us. Help us to discipline our children so they won't be prideful and discontent. Amen

1 King 2:13; 17

Now Adonijah the son of Haggith came to Bathsheba . . .and said, "Please speak to King Solomon for me. .that he may give me Abishag the Shunammite as my wife."

Once again Bathsheba was caught up in an intrigue when her handsome and prideful stepson came to her for help. The request seemed harmless to her, "Ask Solomon if I can marry Abishag."

Abishag was the maiden brought in to keep King David warm in bed while he was dying, and while Bathsheba may have reacted out of kindness to the request, it didn't take Solomon long to decide that this was another of Adonijah's ploys to gain the throne.

Solomon's past disputes with his stepbrother led him to take action. King Solomon declared Adonijah be put to death.

Mother wrote in her journal, **"Life demands action, but it is more than simply reacting. Past victories cannot substitute for present trust."**

Dear Lord, Give us wisdom to know those we can trust. We trust you to guide us. Amen

1 Chronicles 28:20

David said to his son Solomon, "Be strong and of good courage, and do not fear nor be dismayed, for the Lord God – my God – will be with you. He will not leave you nor forsake you until you have finished all the work for the service of the house of the Lord."

In this verse King David gives his son powerful advice based on his own experiences.

In verse 9 the father also told Solomon to have a loyal heart and a willing mind. Any son who follows this advice will be a powerful force for God.

Life is often difficult, but it can be easier if you heed the advice of wise parents.

In her journal Mother wrote, **"Being a Christian involves a lifetime of hard work dedicated study and difficult decisions.**

Dear Lord, Thank you for wise parents who love and guide their children. Help children to listen and heed their advice. Amen

2 Chronicles 7:14

If my people who are called by My name will humble themselves and pray and seek My face, and turn from their wicked ways, then I will hear from heaven and will forgive their sin and heal their land.

Solomon, like his father David, prayed. God, who always listens to His people, heard Solomon and made the promise in this verse.

Humbly seeking God's forgiveness is the first step towards healing, but you can't stop there. You have to quit committing the sin.

If you are a gossip – stop it! If you are a drunk – stop it! If you watch porn – stop it!

God will forgive you and heal you, but you have to stop it!

Mother wrote in her journal, **"Your choices today effect eternity. If God's people follow God's plan they will reap His blessings."**

Dear Lord, Forgive me for the sin of _____, and give me the strength to stop it. Amen

Psalm 46:1

God is our refuge and strength; a very present help in trouble.

A dear friend has a garden at the side of her house that gives special comfort.

Amid the puffy hydrangeas, willowy hollyhocks, and other plants loaded with vibrant blossoms of yellow and purple, stands a bronze angel that reminds my friend of families who have babies in heaven.

She knows from experience that the only comfort that follows such a loss comes from trust in God and faith that one day the families will be complete.

Mother wrote in her journal, **"Even sorrows turn to blessings when they make us less attached to earth and more attached to God"**

Dear Lord, there is so much we don't understand. Comfort the families who have broken hearts. Thank you for the hope of reunions in heaven. Amen

Genesis 12:4

So Abram departed as the Lord had spoken to him, and Lot went with him. And Abram was seventy-five years old when he departed Haran.

A few years ago I came across a book written by a man who felt led by The Lord to carry a cross as he traveled around the world.

God prepared him when as a boy he carried water to the field hands on his father's farm. He never took a straight path. Listening to his heart, he would go right, then straight, then right or left. Whatever direction his heart said take, that's the way he went.

When he undertook his mission to carry the cross, he knew how to listen to the Holy Spirit whose directions eventually lead him safely around the world.

In her journal Mother wrote, **"You may not receive new guidance from God until you have acted on his previous directions."**

Dear Lord, Thank you for the Holy Spirit who guides us if we will listen and obey. Give us courage to follow where you lead. Amen

Exodus 20:3

Thou shalt have no other Gods before me.

In the book of Daniel, Nebuchadnezzar made an image of gold and decreed everyone should worship it. He gave a musical cue and expected everyone to bow down. The king had the power and influence to dictate who the people could worship, but four men had the courage to resist.

We often make our own idols. Power, money, an addiction, another person, a career, status – anything that takes all our time, energy and focus away from The Father can become our idol.

Mother wrote in her journal, **"Whatever holds first place in our lives or controls us is our God. The Lord alone is worthy of our service and worship and we must let nothing rival Him."**

Heavenly Father, We praise you today for loving us so much that you sent your son, Jesus to save us. You alone are worthy of our praise. Amen

Contentment

One morning this week my friend, Donna posted this on Facebook, "Contentment frees you to enjoy every good thing God has given you. Contentment demonstrates your belief that God loves you and has your best interest in mind.—Blackaby."

She went on to say, "I'm so very grateful for the contentment, joy and peace that come from my personal relationship with Jesus Christ!"

Her post caused me to think about the meaning of contentment which brought back some memories of a trip I took to Tybee Island with my oldest daughter and granddaughter.

We enjoyed our time on the island and the two trips into Savannah. We toured the lovely old city and ate at Paula Dean's restaurant.

Following the standard protocol, we left our name with the hostess and received our designated time to return for our meal. We walked a few blocks then returned to browse the Paula Dean shops before joining the buffet line.

Fried chicken, peas, creamed potatoes, an assortment of vegetables and hot breads were piled high on the heated trays and ended at a massive dessert table.

We ate until our appetites were sated, and as we sipped our sweet tea my daughter wiped her mouth and said, "That was amazing, but Grandmother Elizabeth's Sunday dinners were better."

As the granddaughter of a fantastic cook, she was used to southern feasts and was less impressed with Paula's spread.

Mother wrote in her journal, "**Recognize everyday blessings and be thankful. Gratitude opens our hearts to more blessings.**"

Today I will be content and acknowledge my blessings.

Esther 4:14

"For if you remain completely silent at this time, relief and deliverance will arise for the Jews from another place, but you and your father's house will perish. *Yet who knows whether you have come to the kingdom for such a time as this.*"

A lovely teenager was a good student involved in many high school activities. Her principal asked some of the girls in her leadership group to participate in a fashion show. The theme was Appropriate School Attire.

She was anxious because she knew she and the others would be criticized. Her mom gave her some wise advice, "Anybody can take pot shots at the leaders because they are out front. Don't let that stop you. Lead anyway."

Mother wrote in her journal, "**Criticism will always be directed toward those who lead because they are out in front. As you lead, don't spend valuable time and energy worrying about that. Focus on those who are willing to listen and help.**"

Dear Lord, Today we pray for those you have called to leadership positions for such a time as this. Give them spirits of power and love to do your will. Help them to focus on those who will listen. Amen

Proverbs 15:1-2

A soft answer turns away wrath, but a harsh word stirs up anger. The tongue of the wise uses knowledge, but the mouth of fools pours forth foolishness.

If I watch a news channel, I want unbiased news, which is almost impossible to find. It is much easier to find people yelling their opinions at one another. Yelling won't make them right.

Living in a volatile world makes a soft answer unusual, but compelling. God in His wisdom knows this. If you are a person who usually employs a soft answer, people will pay attention when you do raise your voice.

In her journal Mother wrote, **"Anger is a strong emotion. Often it may drive people to hurt others with words or physical violence. But anger directed at sin and the mistreatment of others is not wrong. When injustice or sin makes you angry, ask God how you can channel that anger in constructive ways"**.

Dear Lord, Today we pray for the wisdom that can respond appropriately in any situation. Amen

Judges 13:24

So the woman bore a son and called his name Sampson; and the child grew and the Lord blessed him.

In January I began reading through the Bible. The process is taking longer than I thought it would because after I read a chapter or two, I ponder.

The scriptures reflect a hot mess of humanity who do horrible, despicable things to each other, and reading about them leaves me wondering how God could love them.

Yet he consistently sent people who could make a difference in their lives. Sometimes those sent performed amazing feats – like Sampson. Sometimes, like Abdon, the only noted accomplishment was to have "forty sons and thirty grandsons who rode around on seventy donkeys".

In the Old Testament God cares about these lost ones and in the New Testament he sends Jesus the ultimate proof of that love.

In her journal Mother wrote, **"Taking time for reflection allows us to focus our attention on God's goodness and strengthens our faith."**

Dear Lord, Send your Holy Spirit to reveal the truth in your word and to speak to us as we reflect upon it. Amen

Judges 17:1

Now there was a man from the mountains of Ephriam whose name was Micah.

Micah was a thief who had a desire to worship something. He made his own idols and enlisted a young man to be his personal priest.

At that time, there was no king in Israel and the people did what seemed right to them. Though Micah searched for God he looked in the wrong places. He floundered.

Some days I flounder, but with the help of His Word and the guidance of the Holy Spirit, I can look to the one true God and find my way.

In her journal Mother wrote, **"As you face problems and temptations, focus your attention on God and His assurances –trusting Him to help you."**

Dear Lord, Thank you for stories in the Bible that show us the good and the misguided. Help us to focus on You and trust You for help each day. Amen

Genesis 16:1

Now Sarai, Abram's wife, had born him no children. And she had an Egyptian maidservant whose name was Hagar.

Life is full of choices and Sarai, chose to run ahead of the Lord rather than to wait upon His promise of a child.

Becoming impatient, she devised a plan to let her husband sleep with her servant, Hagar. Hagar became pregnant and no longer felt like a servant since she was carrying Abraham's heir. She tormented Sarai and that made Sarai mad at Abram. The situation became intolerable for Abram and he eventually sent Hagar and her son away.

In her journal Mother wrote, **"When faced with a difficult decision, don't allow impatience to drive you to disobeying God. God often uses delays to test our obedience and patience."**

Dear Lord, What a mess we make when we become impatient and act on our own. Help us to seek Your will and be patient so we make good choices. Amen

Genesis 22:2

And He said, "Take your son, your only son Isaac, whom you love and go to the land of Moriah and offer him there as a burnt offering on one of the mountains of which I shall tell you.

Aside from John 3:16, this verse speaks the loudest to me of sacrifice.

Abraham had waited years for Isaac, the son God promised him with Sarah, yet when God spoke in chapter 22, Abraham obeyed. He trusted God.

How heavy his heart must have been!

A friend was told her twelve year old daughter might have a brain tumor. My friend found the faith to pray, "Lord, you loved her first and you love her best and if this is your will I give her back to you." The many tests that followed showed no tumor.

Some would say the initial speculation was incorrect, but maybe God heard my friend's prayer of faith and stepped in. She trusted God.

Mother wrote in her journal, **"Obedience always involves sacrifice, but sacrifice is not always obedience."**

Dear Lord, Help us to know when you require a sacrifice and give us the faith and strength to trust You. Amen

1 Samuel 15:23

For rebellion is as the sin of witchcraft, and stubbornness is as iniquity and idolatry because you have rejected the word of the Lord, He has also rejected you from being king.

Sometimes you need to plant your feet, shake your head and firmly say, "No, I'm not going to do that!"

But make sure these words aren't spoken to someone who consistently shows he/she has your best interest at heart. Rebelling against godly friends and family members makes it easier to say no to God's calling on your life and brings as much disappointment and trouble as embracing witchcraft or idolatry.

It is sad to see the hearts of godly parents break when grown children rebel against what they were taught growing up.

Mother wrote in her journal, **"Even those who are close to God have moments when they want to escape from their problems and pressures."**

Dear Lord, Thank you for loving us and putting people in our paths who will help guide us to our destiny. Help us run to You, not away from You, when we feel the pressures of life. Amen

Ruth 1:16

But Ruth said, "Entreat me not to leave you or to turn back from following after you. For wherever you go, I will go; and wherever you lodge, I will lodge. Your people will be my people and your God, my God.

Acquaintances might bail when you are broke or broken, but real friends love you - not your circumstances.

Ruth and Naomi developed a bond that started when Ruth married Naomi's son, but their friendship developed after they both became widows. Naomi relied on Ruth's youthful strength and companionship, while Ruth benefited from Naomi's wisdom and experience.

Trusting in God and on each other, they fulfilled the destiny God had for them as Ruth eventually married Boaz and became the great-great grandmother to King David and a direct ancestor to Jesus.

In her journal Mother wrote, **"Nothing hurts more than a wound from a friend. Real friends stick by you in times of trouble and bring healing, love, acceptance and understanding."**

Dear Lord, Thank you for friends who stand by us through thick and thin. Protect and keep them close to Your heart. And Father, we thank you for being the best Friend of all. Amen

Psalm 27:4

One thing I have desired of the Lord. That I will seek: That I may dwell in the house of the Lord all the days of my life; to behold the beauty of the Lord and to inquire in His temple.

Priorities in our lives change, but as Christians our constant priority is "visiting" with Him in His house. Since He owns the whole world, a visit can take place anywhere.

A morning visit might be on the front porch or in the sunroom. At noon I may talk with Him before I eat my lunch and at night I just sleep better if I come into His presence before I doze off.

In all these visits, I have total access to My Father.

In her journal Mother wrote, **"Praying evening, morning and noon is an excellent way to maintain correct priorities throughout every day."**

Dear Father, Thank you for being always accessible and allowing us to bring every care to you. Show us what is most important to you today and help us accomplish it for Your glory. Amen

Are You a Christian?

We went with a group to St John to help a missionary couple who live there. Our mornings were spent working on some projects, but we took advantage of our hosts' knowledge of the island to plan some afternoon outings.

Our first excursion was to a local restaurant overlooking the bay. As we watched the sailboats dance in their moorings, we happily enjoyed a heavenly breeze and some fried key lime pie. After paying my bill, I stuffed the change into my billfold.

There were several shops downstairs and as we window shopped, the reflection of a man appeared beside me. He was tall and thin with braids down his back and a colorful knitted hat covering the top of his head.

In order to move to the next store, I had to step around him and before I could do so he spoke to me in a distinctive island accent,

"Are you a Christian?"

I was caught off guard by his directness but didn't feel the least bit threatened. I paused a moment before answering because I was trying to figure out how he knew. Then I realized I was wearing a cross around my neck and replied, "Yes, I am."

"I am a Christian too!" he said pointing to the cross around his own neck.

"Then you are my brother in Christ," and I was turning to walk on when he said,

"Will you buy me some food?"

Now I had just acknowledged him as my brother (a little flippantly). How could I tell him no? I couldn't so I took his arm intending to go back to the restaurant area we had just left and said,

"Sure. Come with me."

He held back and quietly said, "They won't let me in there anymore."

Well, to make a short story shorter, I adjusted my plan and pressed some money into his hand. He responded by giving me an unexpected hug then turned and walked away.

By wearing my cross I advertised my faith and he responded to my "brand". Maybe experience had shown him that people wearing crosses were easier to approach or maybe his own cross indicated a belief in a fellow faith walker. Either way that brief encounter on St John was a forceful reminder to be what you advertise or you are falsely advertising.

In her journal Mother wrote, **"God controls all events and works His will in them."**

Joshua 23:10

One man shall chase a thousand, for the Lord your God is He who fights for you, as He has promised you.

Though this scripture is about the battles Joshua led with only a few men, it could also apply to what Sampson did to the Philistines.

An angel appeared to Sampson's mother and told her she would have a son. She was to avoid wine and anything unclean while she was pregnant and her son would be raised as a Nazirite (set aside for the Lord and not allowed certain food or drink).

Sampson fulfilled the purpose for which he was born and singlehandedly destroyed thousands of Israel's enemies.

Mother wrote in her journal, **"God is never intimidated by the size of the enemy or the complexity of the problem. With Him there are always enough resources to resist the pressures and win the battle."**

Dear Lord, Sometimes we feel overwhelmed and alone in this world, but help us remember that You are greater than any enemy and with You on our side we can do brave and mighty things. Amen

Genesis 9:4

But you shall not eat flesh with its life; that is its blood.

Reading through the Old Testament often baffles me because there are so many "Do Nots" that seem very strange, but I have learned through the years that everything in the Bible is inspired by the Holy Spirit for our good. If He says, "Do not" then we shouldn't. He has a reason.

Last year The Los Angeles Times reported that a 20 year study found that any amount of red meat decreased your life span, and recent research found that red meat increases the risk of breast cancer. There are toxins in blood, especially from meat that has been processed.

Several studies suggest that if we can't cut out red meat all together, we should minimize the size of the portion and only eat it once or twice a week.

Mother wrote in her journal, **"It was wrong to eat blood because blood represented life and life belonged to God."**

Dear Lord, Thank you for speaking to us through Your Word. Help us to trust You for our spiritual and physical wellbeing. Make us wise in what we allow in to our bodies and minds. Amen

1 Samuel 1:10

And Hannah was in bitterness of soul and prayed to the Lord and wept in anguish.

Hanna went straight to the Lord with her broken heart. While Sarai took matters into her own hands and wound up with a mess, Hannah waited and her prayers for a son were finally answered by the birth of Eli.

When she had weaned her son for whom she had waited for so long, she took him to the temple and loaned him to the Lord for as long as he lived.

She realized what came from God could be safely entrusted back to Him.

In her journal Mother wrote, **"When we turn to God first, we will never have to turn to Him as a last resort."**

Dear Lord, Thank you for allowing us to come to you with our bitter souls. Give us faith to wait for your answer so we don't make a mess of something you can make glorious. Amen

Judges 11: 30-32

And Jephthah made a vow to the Lord and said, "If You will indeed deliver the people of Ammon into my hands, then it will be that whatever comes out of the doors of my house to meet me, when I return in peace from the people of Ammon, shall surely be the Lord's and I will offer it up as a burnt offering. . . .The Lord delivered them into his hands."

The Holy Spirit came upon Jephthah in verse 29 and empowered him for the battle so why did he make this vow?

Maybe he didn't trust God to do what He said so he bargained with the Almighty to gain more favor.

The first person out of Jephthah's house after the victory was his daughter. Some scholars believe he sacrificed her future as a wife and mother by keeping her a virgin in service to Jehovah.

In her journal Mother wrote, **"In the Bible, God never asked people to make oaths or vows; but if they did, he expected them to keep them."**

Dear Father, Vows are serious business. They indicate things that are to happen in the future and the future belongs only to You. Make us careful and true to the vows we make. Amen

1 Samuel 4:10-11

So the Philistines fought and Israel was defeated, and every man fled to his tent. There was a very great slaughter and there fell of Israel thirty thousand foot soldiers. Also the ark of God was captured . . .

There is always competition. Victory most often goes to the side with the most resources and that's not always the good guys. With all our might, we fight the battles put before us and aim for victory. Even when we don't win, God provides according to His will.

In her journal Mother wrote, **"Sometimes ungodly people win battles. Victory is neither guaranteed nor limited to the righteous. God provides according to His will. The timing of God's plans and promises are known only to Him. Our task is to commit our ways to God and then trust Him for the outcome."**

Dear Lord, Thank you for hearing our prayers in these days of trials and confusion. We ask that you guide us in all that we do and we will trust You with the outcome. Amen

1 Samuel 2:12

Now the sons of Eli were corrupt; they did not know the Lord.

The Bible says Eli's sons did not know the Lord, yet their father was a priest and they were raised in a priestly environment.

These sons used their positions of authority to take the offerings brought to the temple to benefit themselves. Eli saw it and did nothing, but more importantly, God saw it.

Sometimes people in authority take advantage of their positions and rather than do what is best for their followers, they line their own pockets. They may at first feel guilty, but the guilt is replaced with pride and they begin to feel entitled to what they steal. God sees.

Mother wrote in her journal, **"Dishonest people soon begin to believe lies they construct around themselves. Then they lose the ability to tell the difference between truth and lies."**

Dear Lord, Protect us from people who take bribes and steal assets that are meant for the good of others. Expose their conduct and turn them from their misguided ways, but more importantly, Lord, keep our motives and actions pure. Amen

1 Samuel 13:8-9

Then Saul waited seven days according to the time set by Samuel. But Samuel did not come to Gilgal; and the people were scattered from him. So Saul said, "Bring a burnt offering and peace offerings here to me." And he offered the burnt offering.

When the Israelites said they wanted a king, God told Samuel to go find Saul and Saul was anointed to fill the position.

As long as God's spirit was on Saul, he was powerful. When a crucial battle was brewing and Samuel didn't show up at the appointed time to offer a sacrifice, Saul took the role he had no business assuming.

Saul's desire to sacrifice came from his fear of failure rather than a love for the Lord.

Mother wrote in her journal, **"A sacrifice was a ritual transaction between men and God that physically demonstrated a relationship between them. But if the person's heart was not truly repentant or if he did not truly love God, the sacrifice was a hollow ritual."**

Dear Lord, Thank you for sacrificing your son, Jesus, on the cross to save us. Forgive us when we presume to try and save ourselves. Amen

1 Samuel 15:10-12

The word of God came to Samuel saying, "I greatly regret that I have set Saul up as king . . . . So Samuel went to meet Saul and was told, "Saul went to Carmel and set up a monument for himself."

If God chooses you for a certain task do it with a humble heart. The minute pride steps in you lose your focus for God's real purpose, and pride often leads to rebellion.

Saul began to arrange sacrifices on his own instead of allowing Samuel to perform that important function. Finally Samuel told him God wanted his obedience not his sacrifice, but by then God had chosen another to be king.

Later in his life, Saul was visited by an evil spirit. Maybe its name was Regret.

In her journal Mother wrote, **"Rebellion against God is perhaps the most serious sin of all because as long as a person rebels, he or she closes the door to forgiveness and restoration with God."**

Dear Lord, Guard us against rebellion that would separate us from You. Amen

Isaiah 30:19-20

He will be very gracious to you at the sound of your cry; When He hears it, He will answer you. . . though the Lord gives you the bread of adversity and the water of affliction. . . .

The father of a friend took a civil servants test and passed with flying colors which put him in line for a promotion. He waited expectantly and was crushed to find out the position went to someone else at the discretion of his supervisor. Though he did not retaliate, he didn't forgive either. His disappointment and anger lasted a life time.

Had he claimed the promise in Isaiah, he might have seen all the many, many blessings the Lord had given him.

In her journal Mother wrote, **"When treated unjustly, we should not take matters into our own hands. God who is faithful and just sees all that is happening and will judge all evil."**

Dear Lord, Thank you for hearing our cries. Protect us from those who treat us unjustly and give us faith to let You judge them. Amen

1 Samuel 16:7

But the Lord said to Samuel, "Do not look at his appearance or at the height of his stature, because I have refused him. For the Lord does not see as man sees; for man looks on the outward appearance, but the Lord looks at the heart."

King Saul was tall, good looking and powerful, but he had a heart problem. His was set on himself and not God. He looked the part, but he was no longer pleasing to God, and His spirit left Saul.

God sent Samuel to anoint another king. Jesse had many sons who were physically appealing, but God wanted one whose heart was set on Him. He chose ordinary looking David and when Samuel anointed him, "the spirit of the Lord came upon him."

In her journal Mother wrote, **"The Lord takes ordinary things and people and does extraordinary things. God often uses simple objects to accomplish His tasks in the world. It is important only that they be dedicated to Him for His use. Anything is a possible instrument for Him."**

Dear Lord, Make us instruments you can use. Amen

1 Samuel 18:8-9

Then Saul was very angry, and the saying displeased him; and he said, "They have ascribed to David ten thousands, and to me they have ascribed but thousands. Now what more can he have but the kingdom. So Saul eyed David from that day forward.

King Saul resented the accolades the women bestowed on David after his battle with the Philistines, and the seed of jealousy was sown in the heart of this powerful man.

Saul had lost favor with God so God had Samuel anoint David to be the next king. The stage was set for envy to grow into hatred which led to attempted murder.

Saul saw David as a rival and sought ways to remove this threat to his power.

In her journal Mother wrote, **"Jealousy my not seem to be a major sin, but in reality it is one step away from murder. Beware of letting jealousy get a foothold in your life."**

Dear Lord, Keep us close to you so that the seed of jealousy won't grow into words or actions we will regret. Amen

Dystopian

We watched an episode of a dystopian series on Netflix with our ten year old grandson. I said, "This is a little dark and pretty intense."

He replied, "It's the times Meme."

Dystopia is a popular genre with young people. *The Hunger Games* is a good example of a dystopian society where propaganda is used to control the citizens. Information, independent thought and freedom are restricted.

Citizens in a dystopian society are under constant surveillance and the society expects uniformity in their effort to create a perfect world. Set in the future, it's a little bit Captain Kirk meets Indiana Jones.

Young people appreciate this genre because the characters face greater challenges then they do in their own lives and the readers identify with the strong, hopeful characters.

My favorite book, the Bible, is full of stories about people who often lived in societies where they were vexed by expectations to give up their freedom and conform to a norm with which they weren't comfortable, and it also speaks of a time in the future that correlates with a dystopian society.

Revelations tells of beasts, identifying numbers tattooed on foreheads; a time when Antichrist rules the world. It sounds heinous to me, but I don't think I'll be here. I feel sorry for those who are.

When I watch dystopian movies, I cheer for the heroes and heroines but I know that their victories are short lived. There never seems to be an end to their peril.

In the book of my faith, there is a happy ending because Christ died on the cross, overcame death and opened the way to everlasting life with God in heaven.

In her journal Mother wrote, "**The person who has no expectations and therefore fails to be on the alert will receive little help. Watch for God in the events of your life. (Streams in the Desert)**

I watch for God, and I expect a happy ending.

1 Samuel 20:30-31

Then Saul's anger was aroused against Jonathan and he said to him, "You son of a rebellious woman! Do I not know that you have chosen the son of Jesse (David) . . . . for as long as the son of Jesse lives on earth, you shall not be established nor your kingdom."

David (God's newly anointed) and Jonathan (heir to Kings Saul's throne) were friends. Even after Saul declared David his enemy, Jonathan remained loyal to David.

Loyalty is the most selfless part of love. To be loyal you cannot live only for yourself.

Loyal people not only stand by those they love, they are willing to suffer for them. Jonathan's loyalty to David may have cost him a kingdom.

In her journal Mother wrote, **"Great friendships are costly because loyalty is one of life's most costly qualities."**

Dear Lord, You are a friend who sticks closer than a brother and that friendship requires our utmost loyalty. Amen

1 Samuel 22: 17

Then the king (Saul) said to the guards who stood about him, "Turn and kill the priests of the Lord, because their hand also is with David, and because they knew when he fled and did not tell it me." But the servants of the king would not lift their hands to strike the priests of the Lord.

Saul became king because God chose him, but Saul pushed God aside and did as he saw fit. The scripture tells us that God sent an evil spirit to Saul.

Sometimes God lets evil develop so we learn its effects; then we are more apt to oppose it. The old saying is true, "Evil flourishes when good people do nothing."

In her journal Mother wrote, **"God does not promise to protect good people from evil in this world, but He does promise that ultimately all evil will be abolished. Those who remain faithful through their trials will experience great rewards in the age to come. (Matt. 5:11-12; Rev 21: 1-7 and 22:1-21)**

Dear Lord, We pray today for wisdom to know which battles are ours. Give us the strength to fight them for Your sake. Amen

1 Kings 12:8

But he rejected the counsel which the elders gave him, and consulted the young men who had grown up with him. . .

Solomon asked God for wisdom, which God gave. Wisdom enabled Solomon to rebuild the temple and prosper his kingdom, but somewhere along the line he realized that all this wisdom was vanity because he would eventually die and all of his wealth would be left to someone else.

When Solomon died, his son, Rehoboam, became king. He foolishly took advice from his peers rather than from the elders who had given his father wise counsel, alienating all but one of the tribes under his rule. Rehoboam's unwise decision opened the door to 400 years of strife, weakness and destruction of his nation.

In her journal Mother wrote, **"Rather than try and undo the results of hasty decisions, we should take time to discern God's will beforehand. We can hear Him speak through the counsel of others, His Word and the leading of the Holy Spirit."**

Dear Lord, Make us wise in our choices. Give us ears that want truth and not just flattery from others and hearts that invite your Spirit's guidance. Amen

1 Kings 13:18-19

He (the old prophet) said to him (the Man of God), "I too am a prophet as you are and an angel spoke to me by the word of the Lord, saying, "Bring him back with you to your house, that he may eat bread and drink water". But he lied to him.

The Man of God had every intention of obeying God's instruction that he go to Jeroboam and express His displeasure at the king's idol worship. Completing his mission, The Man of God refused the king's offer of refreshment only to be waylaid by the lie of someone he thought he could trust.

This passage reminds us to beware of seemingly righteous people Satan uses to lead us astray, and that we too could become false prophets if we don't constantly seek Him through prayer and Bible study.

Mother wrote in her journal, **"Not every opportunity is sent from God. We may want something so much that we assume any opportunity to obtain it is of divine origin. When opportunities come your way, double check *your* motives to make sure you are following God's desires and not just your own."**

Dear Lord, Protect us from Satan's lies. Amen

1 Kings 13:26

So the prophet said, "It is The Man of God who was disobedient to the word of the Lord. Therefore . . . the lion has torn him and killed him."

The Man of God had just met the old prophet whose lie caused him to disobey God's orders. The Man of God didn't know the man's true character which was revealed when he accused The Man of God of disobedience while never acknowledging his own lie.

My friend had a colleague who gave him praise and accolades every time they were together. At first this pleased my friend, but he eventually realized this new acquaintance planned to involve him in something unsavory and then blame my friend if the plan went awry. His Christian witness would have been terribly damaged.

In her journal Mother wrote, **"True friends are more than just companions who enjoy each other's company. They encourage each other's faith in God and trust each other with their deepest thoughts and confidences."**

Dear Lord, Thank you for true friends. Protect us from people who seem to want what's best for us, but are not who they appear to be. Amen

1 Kings 17:22

Then the Lord heard the voice of Elijah, and the soul of the child came back to him and he revived.

God sent the prophet Elijah to stay awhile with a widow and her son. While there, the son got sick and "there was no breath left in him". The widow pleaded with Elijah and Elijah begged the Lord to "let the child's soul come back to him".

Many parents have begged God to heal a child and instead of healing, the child slipped away. The only comfort to a believer is the promise that a precious soul can leave a body and live with the Lord. That promise, and the hope of having new bodies, can take us from total despair and give us strength to endure great losses.

In her journal Mother wrote, **"The same hand that made the beauty of this world has a more beautiful place prepared for us."**

Dear Father, Thank you for the hope of heaven that your word gives us as believers. Comfort every parent who waits to be reunited with a child. Amen

1 Kings 18:4

For so it was while Jezebel massacred the prophets of the Lord, that Obadiah had taken one hundred prophets and hidden them, fifty to a cave, and had fed them with bread and water.

Jezebel, the wife of King Ahab, was a vicious and powerful woman. These traits would have been deadly for the prophets of the Lord if not for Obadiah's bravery.

Few people have ever heard about Corrie ten Boom who hid many Jews and other people during the Nazi occupation of the Netherlands in a room above the family watch shop.

Her brave actions saved over 800 people and resulted in Corrie and her sister being caught and sent to a concentration camp. Her story is told in the book **The Hiding Place.**

Mother wrote in her journal, **"Life's tough situations can bring out the best in people."**

Dear Lord, Thank you for people who find the courage to be noble in desperate situations. When times are tough, help us to act bravely even when we're afraid. Amen

1 Kings 17:9

"Arise and go to Zarephath, which belongs to Sidon, and dwell there. See I have commanded a widow there to provide for you."

The mighty God sent the great prophet, Elijah, to stay with a starving widow and her son. After asking her for some water, he said, "Please bring me a morsel of bread".

Literally down to her last crumb, she and her son faced starvation, and this man expected her to feed him!

She needed a miracle and God used Elijah to provide one. Elijah said, "For thus says the Lord God of Israel: the bin of flour shall not be used up nor the jar of oil run dry until the Lord sends rain on the earth." (That turned out to be three years!).

God provided for her and she provide for Elijah.

In her journal Mother wrote, **"One does not need a prestigious position to play a significant role."**

Dear Lord, Help us to be thankful for whatever position you have given us whether great or small and to do everything You ask us to do even if it seems impossible. Amen

1 Samuel 2:18

But Samuel ministered before the Lord, even as a child, wearing a linen ephod.

Ephods were long, sleeveless vests made of plain linen and were worn by all priests. The high priest's was embroidered with a variety of bright colors. A pouch on the ephod held the Urium and the Thummim, two small objects used to determine God's will. God told His people to use these when consulting him on national issues, and they only gave yes or no answerers.

The Bible often gives examples of leaders seeking God's will before they made monumental decisions, and it's a good example for our nation's leaders to follow.

Prophets eventually replaced these objects of decision making. Now, through Christ, believers have the privilege of going directly to the Father with any problem we have.

Mother wrote in her journal, **"By using the Urium and the Thummim the Israelites were taking important decisions out of their own hands and turning them over to the Lord."**

Dear Lord, Thank you for Jesus who makes it possible, through the Holy Spirit, to come to you for direction in any decisions we make. Help our nation's leaders to seek Your will. Amen

1 Kings 15: 4-5

Nevertheless for David's sake the Lord his God gave him a lamp in Jerusalem by setting up his son . . . . because David did what was right in the eyes of the Lord and did not turn aside from anything He commanded him all the days of his life, except in the matter of Uriah the Hittite.

God called David a man after His own heart not because David was perfect, but because he did what God asked him to do. When he sinned, he repented.

Several years ago the humiliating antics of a national politician caused him to resign. Although he apologized to his wife and the public in general, he eventually returned to politics only to repeat his ridiculous behavior.

Mother wrote in her journal, **"We may make a big show of denouncing sin, but if our hearts do not change the sins will return. Knowing what is right and condemning what is wrong does not take the place of doing what is right."**

Dear Lord, We thank you for the Bible that tells us what we should do. Thank you for forgiving us when we fail and truly repent. Amen

Karma

Recently my long- time friend, Ann Cocktale, called and we had a good visit. She always makes me laugh and it's usually at her expense.

When Ann calls, I mostly listen and laugh, and this conversation was no different.

"Well, I got a great lesson in Karma the other day," Ann began. "Sue Ellen stopped by with my birthday gift. It was in a pink bag and stuffed with about fifteen pieces of rose colored tissue paper. She's so sweet. Well we talked awhile and then she told me to open her present.

I pulled out the paper and inside was a decorative box and inside the box was a lovely silk scarf."

"Aw, that's nice." I injected.

"Yes, it was. I was speechless, actually. That scarf had all my favorite colors in it and would look great with many of my outfits."

Ann paused.

"In fact those were the thoughts I had when I saw it in the mall and bought it for Sue Ellen a couple of years ago on her birthday."

"Are you kidding?"

"Nope, she couldn't have given me anything I liked more. Thus the lesson about Karma: What you give out comes back to you."

"Did you remind her?"

"No, she would be mortified, and besides I really like that scarf."

After we finished our conversation I googled "Karma" and found the word has its origin in Hinduism and Buddhism referring to action seen as bringing inevitable results, good or bad, either in this life or the next. Actually, being rewarded or punished according to ones deeds.

The concept is similar to "Do unto others as you want them to do unto you" or "As you sow so you reap".

The moral of Aesop's fable, The Ant and the Dove, is a good example of Karma in action.

A tiny ant wants a drink of water so she leans over a rushing stream, loses her balance and falls in. The current carries the little insect downstream to where a dove sits on a tree branch.

Seeing the ant's peril, the dove nips a leaf with its beak and tosses it to the ant who hops on the leaf and is saved. She sails to safety.

Later, a hunter sees the kind, fat dove and desires to kill it for dinner. Placing an arrow in his bow, the hunter takes aim, but the tiny ant happens to be nearby and attacks his ankle. The bites distract the hunter and the dove is saved by the actions of the tiny creature.

Obviously, if the dove had not saved the ant the ant could not have later saved the dove.

What goes around comes around.

My faith teaches that we are saved by grace not Karma. God's grace through Christ's sacrifice on the Cross ensures my next life.

Mother wrote in her journal, **"Obedience to our inner conscience brings the power of God into our lives."**

It never hurts to send out the good.

1 Kings 17: 5-6

Elijah went and did just what the Lord said. He stayed by the Cherith Brook that faced the Jordan River. The ravens brought him bread and meat in the mornings and evenings. He drank from the brook. "

By doing what the Lord asked him to do, Elijah put himself in a stressful situation, but the Lord had already prepared a respite for Elijah – water during a time of drought and food delivered by ravens.

I have never been fed by birds, but I have on occasion been under stress and seen Him provide a time of relief. Once He took a meager five dollar bill and provided transportation and a week end of much needed rest.

Though His resources are unlimited, "The Lord of Heavenly Forces" sometimes chooses the simplest ways to minister to us. Accept whatever He offers.

In her journal Mother wrote, **"Let life's difficulty and obstacles push you in God's direction and make you depend upon Him; turning to anything or anyone else leads only to disaster."**

Dear Lord, Today we pray for those who follow you yet find themselves in stressful situations. Send Your Holy Spirit to guide them to a place of respite so they can be refreshed and revived. Amen

1 Kings 3:14

So if you walk in my ways, to keep my statutes and my commandments, as your father David walked, then I will lengthen your days.

There are many instances in the Bible where people facing difficult situations sought direction from the Lord and followed His instructions.

A pastor in our area felt called away from the thriving church he led for almost ten years to become a church planter in another section of the country. Over and over the pastor prayed for guidance and each time the Lord reaffirmed his new calling. The wise young man did what he was asked to do.

In her journal Mother wrote, **"Sometimes people wonder why God does not answer their prayers, but if they do not fulfill the responsibilities He has already given them they should not be surprised when He does not give further guidance."**

Dear Lord, Thank you for hearing our prayers. Help us to hear and heed your answers. Amen

2 Kings 2: 23-24

And as Elisha went up from there to Bethel some youths came from the city and mocked him and said to him, "Go up, you baldhead! Go up you baldhead!" So Elisha turned around and looked at them and pronounced a curse on them in the name of the Lord, and two female bears came out of the woods and mauled forty-two of the youths.

This crowd of young men threw insults at a man of God who knew to whom he belonged and wasn't afraid to face the gang. God heard him and soon the bullies were gone.

The lesson here is: Don't disrespect anyone God has called or there will be serious consequences.

Mother wrote in her journal, **"God cannot tolerate, ignore or excuse sin. For believers, God's holiness gives comfort because as we worship Him we are lifted from the mire of sin. As we believe in Him, we are made holy."**

Dear Lord, Thank you for calling people to do special tasks for you. Protect them from evil. Amen

2 Kings 4: 4-5

"When you come in, you shall shut the door behind you; then pour it (oil) into all those vessels, and set aside the full ones." So she went from him and shut the door behind her and her sons, who brought the vessels to her; and she poured it out.

A creditor was coming to this widow's door threatening to take her sons into slavery so she asked Elisha for help. The man of God asked what she had in her house and she told him she had only a jar of oil. The Lord, through Elisha, gave instructions which enabled her to pay the debt.

My grandmother's favorite scripture says, "I have been young and now I am old, and I have never seen the righteous go hungry or his children begging bread." Hard work and faith got her family through the Great Depression.

In her journal Mother wrote, **"When facing problems, remember it is useless to look for someone to blame or criticize. Instead consider how you can help find a solution."**

Dear Lord, Make us aware of our resources, however meager, and use them in miraculous ways. Amen

2 Kings 5:11

But Naaman became furious and went away and said, "Indeed I said to myself, 'He will surely come out to me and stand and call on the name of the Lord his God, and wave his hand over the place and heal the leprosy.'

Naaman, a general for the King of Aram, had leprosy and took the advice of an insignificant slave to ask the prophet Elijah for healing, but when Elijah told the powerful man what to do Naaman was not pleased with the simple treatment the prophet prescribed.

He eventually put pride aside, did what he was told and was healed.

In her journal Mother wrote, **"Treat those you meet with respect and dignity no matter how insignificant they may seem. You never know how God will use them to help you or haunt you, depending on your response to them.**

Dear Lord, forgive us for thinking too highly of ourselves. Keep us respectful of others and the way You may choose to use them in our lives. Amen

2 Kings 21:6

Also he made his son pass through the fire, practiced soothsaying, used witchcraft, and consulted spiritists and mediums. He did much evil in the sight of the Lord to provoke Him to anger.

This verse refers to King Manasseh who led Israel to do more evil than the enemies the Lord led them to destroy. By the end of his reign, Jerusalem was covered with innocent blood.

Positions of authority are sometimes held by people with a hidden agenda so we have to be prayerful when deciding who to follow. Our society is more willing to accept the perception of truth rather than The Truth.

Mother wrote in her journal, **"There is a difference between following an order with which you disagree and following one you know is wrong. It is never right or ethical to carry out a wrong act, no matter who gives the order or what the consequences may be. Have the courage to follow God's laws above human commands."**

Dear Lord, Help us to be cautious when offering our loyalty to anyone but You. Amen

2 Kings 20:1-2

In those days Hezekiah was sick and near death. Isaiah said to him, "Put your affairs in order, for you shall die". Hezekiah turned his face toward the wall and prayed to the Lord saying, "Remember me now, O Lord, I pray, how I have walked before You in truth and with a loyal heart, and have done what was good in Your sight." And Hezekiah wept bitterly.

Hezekiah was one of the kings who did what was right in the sight of the Lord which means he had a close relationship with Him. Knowing the Lord enriched King Hezekiah's life. When told he would die, he immediately called out to the Lord for comfort.

In her journal Mother wrote, **"If our lives are not the way we want them now, we can't assume that change will come more easily later. When nearing death, we will respond to God the same way we have been responding all along. Coming face to face with death only shows us what we are really like."**

Dear Lord, Thank you for desiring a close relationship with us. Open our hearts to embrace Your life enriching love. Amen

2 Kings 23:25

Now before him there was no king like him (Josiah), who turned to the Lord with all his heart, with all his soul, and with all his might, according to all the Law of Moses; nor after him did any arise like him.

It is a blessing to watch someone live a heroic spiritual life and to know that every decision he or she makes is done prayerfully and with faith in God. Children who see their parents live this way are likely to also have the courage to walk in faith.

In her journal Mother wrote, **"Heroic spiritual lives are built by stacking days of obedience one on top of the other. Like a brick, each obedient act is small within its self, but in time the acts will pile up and a huge wall of strong character will be built – a great defense against temptation. We should strive for consistent obedience each day."**

Dear Father, We thank you for those in our lives who possess true character. Help us to build a life that strengthens the faith of others. Amen

1 Chronicles 18:14

David ruled over all Israel and administered judgment and justice to all his people.

Israel's leader, King David, prayed and listened to the wise instructions of God's prophets. The result is written in the scripture above.

God was in control when David became king, and He is in control every time our country elects a president.

The first president I can remember, Dwight D. Eisenhower, was elected because of his military achievement during WWII. My dad fought in that war and spoke highly of him.

Each of the presidents who followed professed his faith in God and brought unique qualities that shaped our nation into what it is today.

Mother wrote in her journal, **"God's work done in God's way never lacks God's supply of wisdom and energy."**

Dear Lord, Thank you for godly leaders who seek your will and guidance. We pray that you will supply them with all the wisdom and energy they need to do the job. Amen

Friends

Last week's temperatures were unusually cool. All the rain dropped the temperatures, invigorated the greenery and washed away clouds leaving the sky a pristine blue.

With my IPhone tuned to Travis Cottrell's worship channel on Pandora and ear pods appropriately placed, I took a walk with my best buddy and thought only heaven could be more perfect. For today, Utopia was here in my little corner of the world and I was grateful.

Walking provided a time of praise and praise led to gratefulness for faith, family and friends.

Saturday my neighbor came over and as we talked she said, "You know friends are angels from heaven."

Her statement reminded me to be grateful for the friends God has given me, and I do believe real, true friends are a gift.

We've taken several trips this year. On one we made new friends and on the others we traveled with friends we've known awhile. Both trips were wonderful because we traveled with good people.

Life is that way. If you surround yourself with people you get along with, the trip is nicer, and if I were to give advice to a young person, I would say, "Make your life easier by traveling with the best people – preferably of good character and hopefully smart.

Actually, I have several observations I could share about travels.

1. Take care of your body and your car. Both need to be in top shape so you can get to where you want to go.
2. Be either: a good pilot, copilot, navigator or passenger.
3. Keep a good book handy.
4. Drama is rarely needed and never appreciated so avoid it.

5. Keep a journal so you will remember and learn from your trip.
6. Say please and thank you.
7. Take no kindness for granted.
8. Take no insult to heart for long.
9. Be available to help those in need.
10. Say your prayers.

Mother wrote in her journal, **"Like Longfellow's song which was "breathed in the air; then found again in the heart of a friend", ultimate good can come from a kind word or a gentle act."**

Today I will be grateful for the good people in my life.

1 Chronicles 29:12-13

Both riches and honor come from You, and You reign over all. In Your hand is power and might; In Your hand it is to make great and give strength to all. We thank You and praise Your holy name.

King David achieved greatness in battle and amassed a great fortune that he handed down to his son Solomon with instructions to rebuild the temple of God.

Many parents don't have great wealth to hand down to their children, but they have positive traits (integrity, character and faith) that allow the next generation to build on a solid foundation.

Just as Solomon carried out his father's will and continued his legacy, children who inherit integrity, character and faith can continue the kingdom of God.

Mother wrote in her journal, **"God graciously pours out His favor on us because of who He is. He does not regard personal greatness as something to be used selfishly, but as an instrument to carry out His work among His people. The greatness we should desire is to love others as God loves us."**

Dear Lord, Thank you for everything we have and for parents who left legacies of faith and love. Amen

2 Chronicles 5:1

So all the work that Solomon had done for the house of the Lord was finished; and Solomon brought in all the things which his father David had dedicated: the silver and the gold and all the furnishings. And he put them in the treasuries of the house of God.

Solomon had a purpose – to be a wise leader; and a goal – to build the temple of God. He focused on doing what God asked him to do.

I don't know anyone called to build a temple, but I do know people called to build football programs, businesses, challenging classroom environments, families. Their enthusiasm and love for their calling kept their minds focused and their hands busy.

Mother wrote in her journal, **"Temptation quite often comes when a person's life is aimless. If given in to, the sin creates a cycle of suffering that is not worth the fleeting pleasure it offers. Sin is fatal and must be eradicated from our lives."**

Dear Father, Thank you for the plans you have for our lives. Help us to find and do your will and glorify Your name. Amen

2 Chronicles 7:14

If My people who are called by My name will humble themselves and pray and seek My face and turn from their wicked ways, then I will hear from heaven and will forgive their sin and heal their land.

When he dedicated the temple, Solomon knelt before all the congregation of Israel and prayed for the people. Solomon noted in his prayer that sin is inevitable, but later God told him that our repentance ensures His forgiveness.

Knowing this gives me great comfort because I have often run ahead of the Lord and made a mess of things, but God was waiting patiently for me to repent (say sorry and mean it) and turn around. Repenting always calls for "turning around".

In her journal Mother wrote, **"God seems to move slowly at times. Before moving ahead with what seems obvious, first bring the matter to God who alone knows the best timing."**

Dear Lord, Help us to always seek Your perfect will in our lives, but when we mess up we know our repentance ensures Your forgiveness. Thank You! Amen

2 Chronicles 9:8

Then she (the Queen of Sheba) said to the king (Solomon), "Blessed be the Lord your God, who delighted in you, setting you on His throne to be king for the Lord your God! Because your God has loved Israel, to establish them forever, therefore He made you king over them, to do justice and righteousness."

Solomon was a witness to the Queen of Sheba of God's glory. She came with questions and left with the understanding that everything comes from God!

Recently an elderly gentleman lost his home and all his possessions in a flood. When interviewed by a reporter the man testified, "God gave it all to me and He can take it whenever He chooses."

In her journal Mother wrote, "**God is the only source of true happiness because He offers these intangibles that we mistakenly believe can be found on earth: contentment, security, peace and hope for the future. None of these can be found in a job, a human relationship, money, power or positions. They are God's alone to give.**"

Dear Lord, You are the source of everything tangible and intangible, thank you for all You provide for us. Amen

2 Chronicles 13:18

Thus the children of Israel (led by Jeroboam) were subdued at that time; and the children of Judah (led by Abijah) prevailed because they relied on the Lord God of their fathers.

Jeroboam led eight hundred thousand men into battle yet he lost to Abijah who had half as many. Knowing the Lord was with him gave Abijah courage and victory.

I know someone who stood up to an overwhelming number of powerful people because he felt it was what the Lord wanted him to do. Because he turned to the Lord, he had the courage to act on his convictions.

In her journal Mother wrote, **"Fear can paralyze us, but faith and trust in God can overcome fear. If we trust in God we will be free to respond boldly to the events around us."**

Dear Lord, Help us to be bold in our convictions and to overcome any fear we have when called to stand for You. Amen

2 Chronicles 15:15

And all Judah rejoiced at the oath for they had sworn with all their heart and sought Him with all their soul; and He was found by them, and the Lord gave them rest all around.

King Asa did what was right in God's eyes when he destroyed idols and led his nation in a vow to serve God. God's response was "rest all around".

Every Sunday many of God's people around the world gather to offer praise and honor to the King of Kings. It is a weekly renewal of our vow to follow Him. We bring our burdens, offer up our praise; and when we leave there is "rest all around".

Mother wrote in her journal, **"Only in God are we truly safe and secure. Anything else is false security whether you are surrounded by mighty walls of stone, a comfortable home, or a secure job. No one can predict what tomorrow may bring. Our relationship with God is the only security that cannot be taken away."**

Dear Lord, Thank you that we can rest in You, our only true security. Amen

2 Chronicles 20:15

. . . . "Do not be afraid nor dismayed because the battle is not yours but God's."

Sometimes, like the people of Judah, we have to be reminded that God has our backs.

A small group gathered for prayer and Bible study when one of the women shared a hurtful situation involving her daughter-in-law.

After sharing, my friend asked that we pray for this person who seemed to despise her, "I know God's got this. I just need to pray that He will work it all out and that what I say and do will help and not make everything worse."

Mother wrote in her journal, **"Feelings of bitterness and resentment that go unchecked will destroy a relationship."**

Dear Lord, Strengthen our relationship with You so that our desire is to pray for those who hurt us and allow a true healing in that situation. Amen

Ezra 1:5

. . . All those whose spirits God had stirred up, arose to go up and build the house of the Lord which is in Jerusalem.

Jerusalem had been totally destroyed and its survivors sent into slavery when Cyrus, king of Persian, was stirred by the Holy Spirit to rebuild the temple.

In recent years, a small country church saw its congregation dwindle to a handful. God stirred the spirits of members in a large city church, and a group there began worshiping with the rural congregation. Their decision literally rebuilt that church and it now thrives.

People who are stirred by the Spirit make a difference in the kingdom of God by doing things that seem improbable or even impossible.

Mother wrote in her journal, **"If the Christian life seems ordinary, you may need the Spirit to stir you up. Everyday offers a challenge to live for Christ.**

Dear Lord, when your Spirit stirs our hearts to action, we know you always provide the means to accomplish the task. Thank you! Amen

Nehemiah 8:1-3

Now all the people gathered together as one; and they told Ezra the scribe to bring the Book of the Law of Moses, which the Lord had commanded Israel . . . and he read from it. . . . .

I recently came upon this quote, "The law has two functions: on the positive side it reveals the nature and will of God and shows people how to live. On the negative side, it points out people's sins and shows them that it is impossible to please God by trying to obey all His laws.

Faith is the only way to be saved; the law shows how to obey God in grateful response. Faith does not annul the law; but the more we know God, the more we see how sinful we are. Then we are driven to depend on our faith in Christ alone for salvation.

Mother wrote in her journal, "**The law teaches us the need for salvation; God's grace gives us that salvation.**"

Dear Lord, Thank You for Christ who took our sins to the cross and provided the grace that gives us salvation. Amen

Psalm 42:5

Why are you cast down, O my soul and why are you disquieted within me? Hope in God, for I shall yet praise Him for the help of His countenance.

God is always watching out for His people. He placed Esther in the palace and used her to save a whole nation. He reigns eternally.

We may not be used to save a whole race of people, but we might be asked to make a choice that saves one person.

Sean and Leigh Ann Tuohy took Michael Oher from the bleakness of the ghetto and made him part of their family. In the process they were all blessed and, after playing football at the University of Mississippi, Michael is now living his childhood dream of being in the NFL.

In her journal Mother wrote, **"Christ will reign for eternity – now in His spiritual kingdom and in heaven, and later on earth in the new Jerusalem."**

Dear Lord, from everlasting to everlasting You reign in the lives of Your people. We desire to be used for Your glory. Amen

His Truth Will Be Your Shield

Running ahead of the calendar, the school district for one of our grandsons had their Spring break two weeks ago, and we got to enjoy a visit from him.

The weather was typical for early March requiring us to spend Monday and Tuesday inside playing Monopoly and watching movies. One was the action packed Captain America.

This WW I hero has an experience that enhances his abilities and extends his life to the present time. He possesses a special shield that rests in a holster on his back at the ready should he need protection from an enemy assault.

Wednesday, the weather was perfect for a trip to Union City and a visit to Discovery Park of America. It is aptly named. We made a multitude of discoveries about outer space, the sinking of the Titanic, the military, vintage automobiles, geology and ecology. We only had a day so we will make more discoveries another time.

Thursday was rainy, and we decided to spend it inside Butler's Antique store hunting for treasures.

Before picking up my friend who joined us, I told the grandson that I felt comfortable letting him roam freely in the antique store and challenged him to search high and low until he found something special for the money he had in his pocket.

Taking my advice, he burst through the front door like Indiana Jones looking for the lost tomb. When he resurfaced twenty minutes later, he was the proud owner of some impressive loot and money to spare. Apparently he'd done a little haggling with the proprietor.

Tired and hungry after our adventure, we took a lunch break and googled his find. It was selling on EBay for twice what he paid.

We finished lunch and decided we had the time and money for another search for loot, and at our final stop he unearthed the Captain America shield. Our outing was a success and we headed home.

The rest of the break sped by. I sat down for my quiet time the following Monday and read Psalms 91:4,

"His truth shall be your shield".

Images of Captain America flashed through my mind. Raising his magnificent shield, he warded off any attack. Throwing it, he knocked out foes. Resting in the holster, it protected his back. Just knowing he possessed such a weapon gave him confidence.

In His infinite wisdom, our heavenly Father provided each of his children a shield of protection. With His Word of Truth we can withstand any attack launched against us.

In her journal Mother wrote, **"Doing the impossible is everyday business with God."**

Job 42:10

And the Lord restored Job's losses when he prayed for his friends. Indeed the Lord gave Job twice as much as he had before.

God allowed Job, a good man, to lose all his children and everything he owned. To add insult to injury, his friends spoke judgment to him rather than compassion.

When bad things happen, we want to blame someone. Blame causes guilt and guilt keeps us from seeking God when we need Him the most.

A precious family lost a teenage daughter in a car accident that also severely injured their younger son. Recently the father wrote, "Our Lord and Savior, Jesus Christ, will not forsake you when you are in need of His love and grace. Only by sending *you* His comforters and love can anyone endure this kind of valley experience in their lives. If you ever wonder how God uses you to do His work, it's in your words of comfort, and you probably don't even realize it."

In her journal Mother wrote, **"Each time we show compassion, our character is strengthened."**

Dear Lord, Give us hearts of compassion for those who suffer loss. Amen

Psalms 19:14

Let the words of my mouth and the meditation of my heart be acceptable in Thy sight, O Lord, my strength and my redeemer.

In a world full of angry people, words can trigger an explosion, but sometimes they can serve as a calming salve that diffuses a tense situation.

An Atlanta elementary school bookkeeper, Antoinette Tuff, called 911 and then, for almost 25 minutes, stayed on the line, relaying what a would-be shooter was doing and saying. Her sweet words and demeanor convinced the young man to give himself up to authorities instead of going on a shooting spree inside the school.

Mother wrote in her journal, **"Often we respond angrily and defensively rather than trying to diffuse the other person's anger. Instead of fighting, we should seek peace."**

Dear Lord, Give us wisdom each day to act in a way that pleases you and soothes angry situations. Help us seek peace. Amen

Psalm 27:13-14

I would have lost heart, unless I had believed that I would see the goodness of the Lord in the land of the living. Wait on the Lord; be of good courage, and He shall strengthen your heart. Wait, I say, on the Lord.

A man of faith had been employed by an organization that overextended its resources and went under. Though my friend could draw unemployment, he wanted to be busy so he went to the local mall and walked into the manager's office at a national retailer. He walked out with a job in the camera department.

After a short time, he was Salesman of the Week; then Salesman of the Month and before he left for a wonderful job in his chosen field, he was Salesman of the Western Division. He relied on the goodness of the Lord and his faith grew.

In her journal Mother wrote, **"We should use our minds and resources to obey God, while at the same time trusting God for the outcome."**

Dear Lord, Help us to adjust to changes in our lives by using the talents and resources You give us. Thank you for the plans You have for us. Amen

Psalm 60:1

O God, You have cast us off; You have broken us down; You have been displeased; Oh, restore us again!

The little boy had a mop of curly hair and an infectious laugh. He was in church every Sunday and saw his family's faith walk. Yet as a young adult he began to make poor choices that led to addiction and prison.

He was broken down by his addictions, but he can be restored.

In her journal Mother wrote, **"We may be forgiven by God for our sins, but we will often experience harsh consequences."**

Dear Lord, Thank you for Your love that welcomes us back, but make us strong against temptation so we don't wander off in the first place. Amen

Psalm 60:11

Give us help from trouble for vain is the help of man.

Frequent moves while our children were young actually kept them closer to us. Because of new surroundings, school and football games, there was little time for interaction with their peers.

Our final move came when our oldest was in middle school. I knew we were going to be planted awhile and was anxious for her to make friends. When she declined an invitation to a party in the neighborhood, I was disappointed and fussed at her for not going.

Many years later she told me her reason for declining the invitation. She had made a wise choice.

In her journal Mother wrote, **"Ask God in earnest prayer to help you stay away from people, places and situations that may tempt you."**

Dear Lord, Give us wisdom in our choice of friends. There are temptations all around us, but we pray for spirits that flee from anything that would take us away from you. Amen

Psalm 61:1-2

Hear my cry, O God; attend to my prayer. From the end of the earth I will cry to You when my heart is overwhelmed.

When a friend found herself in a situation that caused her to doubt her faith, she fought back. During sleepless nights she would grab her Bible, turn to the Psalms and pray through them.

She even wrote some of the verses on chairs she painted and used in her kitchen, and when she found herself becoming anxious, she recited one of those scriptures.

She later laughed and said, "Instead of standing on the promises I was sitting on them."

Claiming the scriptures kept her from feeling overwhelmed.

Mother wrote in her journal, **"Memorize and meditate on portions of scripture that combat your specific weaknesses. At the root of most temptations is a real need or desire that God can fill, but we must trust His timing."**

Dear Lord, Thank you for Your Word we can count on to bring us through times of temptation. Amen

Psalm 78:35

Then they remembered that God was their rock, and the Most High God their redeemer.

Recently I heard a professional athlete talk about the influence his father had on his life. He ended by saying. "He's more than my dad; he's my friend."

That reminded me of watching a young man struggle through the loss of an infant son. This guy had found the Lord during high school and committed to be a faith walker.

The death of his son shook him, but he sought the council of an older and wiser man whose words of comfort and wisdom not only helped him through a difficult time, but also strengthened his belief in a loving God.

In her journal Mother wrote, **"Find another believer with whom you can openly share your struggles, and call this person for help when temptation strikes."**

Dear Lord, Thank you for the wisdom of faithful elders who will comfort those who hurt. Help us seek the help of Your people when we struggle with temptations. Amen

Psalm 94: 17

Unless the Lord had been my help, my soul would soon have settled in silence.

Just as fire refines silver in the smelting process, trials refine our character. They bring us a new and deeper wisdom and help us discern truth from lies and give us discipline to do what is right.

Above all, trials help us realize life is a gift from God to be cherished; not a right to be taken for granted.

In her journal Mother wrote, **"Billy Graham: Comfort and prosperity have never enriched the world as much as adversity. Out of pain and problems have come the sweetest songs, the most poignant poems, the most gripping stories and inspiring lives."**

Dear Lord, Thank you for Your mercy that holds us up when we go through adversity. Help us turn our trials into stories of faith that inspire others. Amen

Psalm 94:16-19

If I say, "My foot slips!" Your mercy, O Lord, will hold me up. In the multitude of my anxieties within me Your comforts delight my soul.

The years I taught sixth and seventh grade language arts were some of the most rewarding years of teaching. Middle school teachers have to be solid because the emotions of the students are so fluid.

My sixth grade reading classes were full of scrawny little boys dragging around huge feet they would eventually grow into and little girls who were either embarrassed about having a figure, wishing they had a figure or obsessed with showing off what they had recently acquired.

There was an excess of social anxiety, and hurtful words were hurled in a heartbeat; most of the time it was to hide the pitcher's feeling of envy and insecurity.

In her journal Mother wrote, **"The qualities we condemn in others are often our own character flaws. You may discover that in condemning others, you have been condemning yourself"**

Dear Lord, Be with us in the changes of life that make us uncomfortable. Help us to trust You in every stage of our lives.

Psalm 103:1 and 4

Bless the Lord, O my soul and all that is within me bless His holy name! (He) redeems your life from destruction, and crowns you with loving kindness and tender mercies.

When my granddaddy walked down the aisle during a revival, he changed. For years he had been the town drunk, but after that service he never touched another drop and spent the rest of his life trying to make up for his lost years.

No matter how good he became, he always carried the regrets from his past. Mother once told me she would give anything to have memories of a father who took her to church. Though she was thrilled with his repentance, she paid a price for his past behavior.

Mother wrote, **"When God forgives us and restores our relationship with Him, He doesn't eliminate all the consequences of our wrong doing. We may be tempted to say,"If this is wrong I can always apologize to God." But we must remember that we may set into motion events with irreversible consequences."**

Dear Lord, Lead us away from temptations and keep evil from us so we won't harm the lives of others. Amen

Life is Short

When I was little, all the really great events required me to wait. Dessert came after a meal. Movies were watched on Saturdays. Christmas came in December.

The arrival of my teen years required more waiting for the five minutes in the halls between classes to socialize, Friday night ballgames and senior year.

When I got older, I didn't wait for anything if I could help it. I was a young bride and a young mother who grew up with her husband and her kids. I wouldn't change a thing.

Life eventually trained me to more gladly embrace these interludes of anticipation, but I still hate to wait. "Aging up" hasn't given me any more patience.

Mark Twain stated the same feeling when he wrote, "Life is short. Break the rules. Forgive quickly, Kiss slowly, Love truly. Laugh uncontrollably and never regret anything that makes you smile."

Actually that sentiment is Biblical, I think. In 1 Thessalonians 5, Paul says almost the same thing to new Christians who were breaking most of the rules of their society which made "life is short" their reality.

Eight years ago a dear friend and boss was taken suddenly as she shared a morning walk with the love of her life. In a minute her sweet spirit was gone, but she left such precious memories because she realized life is short.

In her journal Mother wrote, **"When we put God first, the wisdom He gives will enable us to have richly rewarding lives."**

My friend led a richly rewarding life. I'm thinking that's the only way to do it.

Psalm 119:92

Unless Your law had been my delight, I would then have perished in my affliction.

A mother whose eighteen year old son died in a car crash became angry at God and doubted His love and mercy.

Years later she told me this story: "Though I was angry with God, after a while I missed Him. On a trip to visit our parents, I issued God a challenge, "God, if you're real then when we get to the next railroad crossing I want You to show me an elephant and a giraffe.

I know it sounds silly, but we had seen a coyote and a few deer at this particular spot before.

When we reached the spot, not a giraffe or elephant was in sight, but on the way back, as we approached the railroad crossing a livestock truck in front of us threw on brakes. The load shifted and there, in the spaces, appeared two wooden forms. One was an elephant and one a giraffe. My journey back to Him had begun."

Mother wrote, **"We can't always control our ups and downs, but we can trust God to help us through our trials. In the end He will reward us.**

Dear Lord, Comfort those parents who have lost children. Carry them until they can trust again. Amen

Psalm 124:2-3

If it had not been the Lord who was on our side when men rose up against us, then they would have swallowed us alive when their wrath was kindled against us.

My dad loved to watch boxing. He would anxiously wait for a match to be aired and then sit in front of the TV weaving and jabbing with the boxers.

One of the most famous boxers of that time was Muhammad Ali. He taunted his opponents unmercifully and would say anything to enhance his own image while psyching out his opponent. His purpose was to gain the advantage and obtain the winner's purse.

We have an opponent who accuses us. Our opponent slings lies and causes us to doubt ourselves and others. His purpose is to steal our joy now and for eternity. Jesus, our defender, is always on our side.

In her journal Mother wrote, **"Don't be hasty to accept someone's condemnation of another, especially when the accuser may profit from the others downfall."**

Dear Lord, Thank you for always having my back when lies are told about me, and help me to refuse to spread lies about others.

Psalm 130:3

If You, Lord, should mark iniquities, O Lord, who could stand?

When I was a young wife and mother, I became friends with two women who loved to show up at my house for coffee after they had taken their kids to school.

My three children were younger and still at home. Coffee at my house was sipped among strewn toys and breakfast dishes. That was fine with me, but I later found out that my clutter was fodder for gossip around the neighborhood.

I decided I was too busy for coffee anyway and I changed morning coffee visits to occasional afternoon tea when the kids napped and the house was tidier.

In her journal Mother wrote, **"Maintaining your composure in the face of unjust criticism can be a trying experience and an emotional drain; but if you can't stop criticism, it is best to ignore it. Remember God knows what you are enduring, and He will vindicate you if you are in the right."**

Dear Lord, Thank you that I am righteous in your sight because of Jesus Christ. Let me give grace to others and leave vindication to you. Amen

Psalm 140: 4-5

Keep me, O Lord, from the hands of the wicked; preserve me from violent men who have purposed to make my steps stumble. The proud have hidden a snare for me, and cords. They have spread a net by the wayside; they have set traps for me.

Living in fear is a terrible way to exist, but naivety isn't the answer.

A beautiful young woman of faith fell in love with a handsome young man who told her exactly what she wanted to hear. She had no experience with liars and cheats so she failed to realize that to him, she was a pawn in his game of deceit.

They were married before she fully understood that his purpose was to trap and destroy her with cruel words and actions that demeaned everything she loved.

Relying on her faith she loaded her car and fled.

In her journal Mother wrote, **"It is only the love of God that can deliver us from the fear of man."**

Dear Lord, Give us the wisdom we need to avoid the snares of the evil one. Amen

Proverbs 1: 7

The fear of the Lord is the beginning of knowledge, but fools despise wisdom and instruction.

Helping with the children's program at our church allows me to meet with a group of first and second graders whose parents' are committed to the spiritual growth of their children.

When we believe that God, in his perfection, never changes then we are anchored in a constantly changing world.

These parents are teaching their kids to base choices on the wisdom of biblical truths instead of worldly opinion. As they grow older their choices have greater consequences; possibly making them targets of those who despise the instruction they received.

 But as Mother wrote in her journal, "**One plus God is a majority. If God is on our side, no one can stand against us (Rom. 8:31).**"

Dear Lord, Thank you for the truth of Your word, and for parents who teach it to their children. Amen

Proverbs 1: 8-9

Hear the instruction of your father, and do not forsake the law of your mother; for they will be graceful ornaments on your head and chains about your neck.

When two little boys got into an argument that resulted in a wrestling match, their mom pulled them apart, heard both sides and instructed the guilty guy to say, "I'm sorry."

Sincerity was not the issue. The words needed to be spoken for the relationship to heal.

A player on a sports team often acknowledges his/her error by saying, "My bad", before doubling the effort required to win.

Our heavenly Father wants us to say sorry, and he wants us to truly repent.

Mother wrote in her journal, **"God hears and forgives us when we pray if we are willing to trust Him and turn from sin. Our desire to forsake our sin must be heartfelt and sincere. Then He will give us a fresh start and a desire to live for Him."**

Dear Lord, Help us to listen and heed Your words of wisdom. Forgive us when we sin and help us turn away from those sins. Amen

Ecclesiastes 2:3

I searched in my heart how to gratify my flesh with wine while guiding my heart with wisdom and how to lay hold on folly till I might see what was good for the sons of men to do under heaven all the days of their lives.

Recently an Ivy League college made the choice to ban alcohol from their campus. Students were interviewed and most seemed surprised that it had taken the administration so long to address the problem.

Pop culture portrays keg parties and binge drinking as a normal part of college life, but according to data from the Center for Collegiate Mental Health, 56 percent of students don't engage in this behavior. If you choose not to drink then you are in the majority.

It is wise to make choices that positively affect your future and if you know drinking can cause negative effects don't participate. Other people may be waiting for you to make a wise choice.

Mother wrote in her journal, **"Little decisions we make are important because they prepare us to make the right choice when the big decisions come. The wisdom to make right choices in all matters is a gift from God."**

Dear Lord, Give wisdom to your people. Help us make wise choices that will positively affect our futures and glorify Your name. Amen

Ecclesiastes 2:9

So I became great and excelled more than all who were before me. Also my wisdom remained with me.

Most of us have heard a sad story about a person with great ability doing something unwise and losing a golden opportunity. Though sad, these stories make great life lessons, but there are probably more stories like the one in the verse above.

It may sound a little bold, but the writer understands that some people are born with more than others. Life is like that. If you have been blessed, praise the Lord and take advantage of every opportunity that comes your way, and don't listen to those who may be jealous.

In her journal Mother wrote, **"Don't ask God to do for you what He wants to do through you. Ask Him for the wisdom to know what to do and the courage to follow through on it."**

Dear Lord, Show me what you want to do in my life. Give me wisdom to use every talent and gift I have. Amen

Ecclesiastes 3:1

To everything there is a season and a time for every purpose under heaven.

This winter we spent a week on Sanibel Island. Every morning the ocean tossed ashore a smorgasbord of marine life for us to admire and treasure.

One morning instead of taking the offerings on the beach, I wandered into the surf where several sand dollars floated ashore.

I am of an age to know what treasures they are. The ones I grabbed in my youth crumbled and vanished. I assumed they would last forever, but nothing does so sometimes it's better to wait for a blessing until the right season of life and appreciate its purpose more.

In her journal Mother wrote, **"Knowledge is good but there is a vast difference between knowledge (having facts) and wisdom (applying the facts to life)."**

Dear Lord, You are so generous with Your blessings. Give me the wisdom to use them for Your glory and not to waste a single one. Amen

Ecclesiastes 3:10

I have seen the God-given tasks with which we are to be occupied. He has made everything beautiful in its time.

After I retired from teaching, I volunteered for a local organization and tutored adults who wanted to get a GED. Two young men were particularly industrious since they realized an education was necessary to make their lives better.

One day as part of their assignment we read nonfiction books about different careers. Afterward I ask them what their ideal job would be.

Tony answered, "I'd like to work somewhere I could meet and talk to lots of people."

Justin shook his head and said, "There's no ideal job. You do whatever you can find for the money to pay your bills."

There was some wisdom in both answers.

Mother wrote in her journal, **"People are happiest when they have joy in whatever their hands find to do. They give their best effort at work because they know God provided the opportunity."**

Dear Lord, Give us jobs so that we may provide for ourselves and our families, and give us an attitude of gratitude as we do those tasks required of us.

Purpose

One of the best things about reading a good book is seeing the results of the characters' choices while watching the consequences of those choices unfold in a matter of hours. Talented authors leave us pondering those choices as well as our own.

If *And the Mountains Echoed*, by Khaled Hosseini, had not been chosen by our book club this month, I would not have read it since, for some reason that I can't remember, I never finished Hossenini's first book, *The Kite Runner*, but last night I finished his last book and I am pondering.

The author drew me in with an interesting fable that foreshadowed the first choice in the book – a father's decision to sell his young daughter to a wealthy woman. The rest of the story weaves through the lives of an excess of characters and back to the woman the little girl became.

Three other characters at different times in the story find themselves responsible for the personal needs of someone who has become unable to care for themselves, and each must choose between personal freedom or the responsibility of another. One caregiver makes this observation,

"They say, 'Find a purpose in your life and live it'. But sometimes it is only after you have lived that you recognize your life had a purpose and likely one you never had in mind, and now that I have fulfilled mine, I feel aimless and adrift."

During 2013 many of my friends took on the responsibility of caring for another person and in doing so they gave up much of their personal freedom. Their situations ranged from sick babies, a loved one with cancer, a son confined to a wheel chair because of a car wreck or spouses with dementia.

Each one stepped up to the plate with courage and grace. They may have had doubts in private moments, but their public faces were (are) noble.

A friend and I recently visited the home of Mother's dear friends, Mr. Ted and Ms Dot. Married for sixty years, he and their daughter make sure "Ma" since she can no longer care for herself.

There is a new wheel chair ramp from the sidewalk to their front door, but it isn't for Ma. It is for their daughter's twenty year old son who is paralyzed from his waist down; the result of a car wreck. During our visit there were jokes and laughter, family stories, chocolate and a peace that really does pass understanding.

Mother wrote in her journal, **"There is a reward (or purpose) for every sorrow; and the sorrow itself is the reward (or purpose)."**

I pray for His wisdom in making the kinds of choices that fulfill my purposes, and glorify Him.

Ecclesiastes 7:1

A good name is better than precious ointment and the day of death than the day of one's birth.

One of the biggest challenges when you enter school for the first time is learning the rules and the consequences that result when those rules are broken. Mastering self-discipline also helps master the academics so the following year is easier.

Each year built on the success of the previous year helps form a reputation as someone who can be trusted with important tasks. Add to that a personal relationship with Jesus and you have a blueprint for success.

In her journal Mother wrote, **"Self-discipline is a responsibility that goes with the privilege of leadership."**

Dear Lord, Thank you for parents, teachers and coaches who care enough about us to instill discipline in our lives. Help us to accept discipline and become people whose end days are better than our beginnings. Amen

Ecclesiastes 7:8

The end of a thing is better than its beginning and the patient spirit better than the proud in spirit.

It is obvious to most people that *practice makes perfect* but somehow, in my childhood, I failed to understand the importance of practicing a skill. Many things came easily to me and if they didn't, I often went on to something else.

For twelve years my sweet mother made sure I took piano lessons, but I never practiced what I learned. Because I was fairly good a sight reading, I got by, but I might have been a talented pianist if I had devoted time to repetition.

It seems ironic that I married a coach whose life was devoted to practice. Without effective practice, the teams were doomed.

There are very few worthwhile things in life that are easily mastered. Practice really does make things perfect so that the end of a thing is better than its beginning.

In her journal Mother wrote, **"Great happiness is found in developing a skill that enhances your life or the lives of others. "**

Dear Father, You are so gracious to give us talents we can enjoy. Help us to hone those skills into opportunities that will glorify Your name. Amen

Job 5:7

Man is born to trouble as sure as sparks fly upward.

My childhood was full of dear sweet people who instilled in me the conviction that I was loved. Feeling loved is the basic requirement for being mentally healthy. Yet even with that security, I often behaved in ways that, I'm sure, troubled my parents.

My belief in a God who loves me gives me confidence, yet I'm often surprised by troublesome situations that cause me to worry and lose focus of that very love, but according to this scripture, trouble shouldn't be unexpected.

When you wake up, thank God for a new day and pray for wisdom and strength to tackle anything that comes along.

In her journal Mother wrote, **"One of God's greatest promises is that beyond the crisis (trouble) lies heaven."**

Dear Lord, We live in a troublesome world. Thank you for being a friend that sticks closer than a brother and for giving us the hope of heaven. Amen

Ecclesiastes 9:9

Live joyfully with the wife (husband) of your choice all the days of your vain life which He has given you under the sun . . for this is your portion in life and in the labor which you perform under the sun.

The only way you can live joyfully is to have Jesus in your heart. There is no joy without Him. Surround yourself with people of joy - people confident in who they are and who see the best in you.

Avoid gossips, gripers and those who are always discontent.

Pick a profession that allows you to positively impact the lives of others then pray that God will put people in your path that can help you achieve your destiny.

Once you have prayerfully made these major choices, live joyfully! That's your testimony to His faithfulness in your life.

Mother wrote in her journal, **"God's will is the most hopeful, pleasant and glorious thing in the world."**

Dear Lord, Give us the wisdom to wisely pick friends and associates who bring out the best in us. Amen

Ecclesiastes 12:14

For God will bring every work into judgment, including every secret thing whether it is good or whether it is evil.

Secrets are hard to keep. As a sixty-four year old man, he looked back at his life with a sickening sadness. The choices he made were all bad. His friends were gone and there was no possibility of sharing his life with someone he loved.

He became physically dependent on others for his basic needs. A friend began tenderly counseling him and uncovered an incident of sexual abuse when he was five. A perverse person basically stole his future.

Mother wrote in her journal, **"The attacks of Satan through the perversion of others can destroy lives if unattended, but if we seek godly council those attacks can be transformed into blessings along the way."**

Dear Lord, There is perversion in our world and children are most often the victims. Deliver us from evil, and when it is in our power, give us the guts to fight it. Amen

Isaiah 1:18

Come now and let us reason together says the Lord. Though your sins be as scarlet they shall be as white as snow.

C. S Lewis' book *The Lion, The Witch and the Wardrobe* was one of my favorite books to read with middle school students.

I discovered this jewel when I took a children's literature class in college, and fell headlong into the magical land of Narnia where I longed to bury my head in Aslan's (the Lion) thick mane while riding upon his strong back.

When he made the ultimate sacrifice for an unworthy Edmund, my heart broke. When he overcame the dark magic of the evil witch, I rejoiced.

Through this work of fiction, C. S. Lewis showed his readers that salvation lies in sacrifice. In reality, my salvation comes from the sacrifice Jesus made for me on the cross and now my sins are as white as snow. I gave nothing and He gave all.

Mother wrote in her journal, **"The gift of greatest worth has no price tag. It is the gift of salvation offered freely by God."**

Dear Lord, Thank you for your Son, Jesus, who died on the cross for my sin. Give me opportunities to talk about what You did for me and by your Holy Spirit lead others to you. Amen

Isaiah 6:8-9

Also I heard the voice of the Lord saying, "Whom shall I send and who will go for us?" Then I said, "Here am I. Send me."

Long ago Mother made sure I faithfully attended Girl's Auxiliary (GAs) a girls' mission group that met every Wednesday night at church where we learned about the wonderful work of home and foreign missionaries.

My heart was especially soft for the stories of the work in Africa, and I felt a pull to spend my life helping people in foreign lands come to know His love. As I grew older and busier with high school, college and later marriage and a family I saw plenty of work to be done close to home.

In my thirties, with a husband and three kids, I began teaching in a Christian school in Gardenia, California. The amazing thing, to me, was that the Sunday night before school started the next day, the church held a commissioning service for the new teachers.

All those years later, the Lord allowed me to fulfill my childhood dream of being a missionary.

In her journal Mother wrote, **"When God places a burden on you, He places His arms underneath you"**

Dear Lord, Thank you for allowing us to be your hands and feet in this world. Help us to seek your will and trust You for guidance. Amen

Isaiah 7:9

If you will not believe, surely you will not be established.

There are lessons to be learned in everyone's life – what to do and what not to do.

I learned many life lessons from a little boy who was born into a family that had a close relationship with the Lord. Every night his family read a Bible verse together then said their prayers before going to sleep.

The mother faithfully took the little boy to church, where he personally committed himself to Christ, but his adult life was never established in faith.

He chose not to live the committment, and he consistently made poor choices. After one especially devastating decision he heard the Lord say, "I cannot bless this stupidity."

Mother wrote in her journal, **"When people ignore God's commands, negative consequences result."**

Dear Lord, Thank you for making the choice to go to Calvary for my sins. Please send Your Holy Spirit to open the hearts of lost people so their lives may be established in Your love. Amen

Isaiah 7:9

If you will not believe, surely you will not be established.

There are lessons to be learned in everyone's life – what to do and what not to do.

I learned many life lessons from a little boy who was born into a family that had a close relationship with the Lord. Every night his family read a Bible verse together then said their prayers before going to sleep.

The mother faithfully took the little boy to church, but he never personally committed himself to Christ so his adult life was never established in faith.

He chose not to believe, and he consistently made poor choices in every aspect of his life. After one especially devastating decision he heard the Lord say, "I can't bless this stupidity."

Mother wrote in her journal, **"When people ignore God's commands, negative consequences result."**

Dear Lord, Thank you for making the choice to go to Calvary for my sins. Please send Your Holy Spirit to open the hearts of lost people so their lives may be established in your love. Amen

Isaiah 30: 1

"Woe to the rebellious children," says the Lord. "Who take counsel, but not from Me, and who devise plans but not of My Spirit that they may add sin to sin."

Last night our eleven year old grandson spent the night with us. We were watching a movie together and a puzzling situation from the script prompted me to ask him his opinion.

He replied, "I don't really know, but my parents don't agree with it so they probably have good reasons."

As Christians, his parents seek truth in His word, the Bible. Everything He asks us to do is for our well-being and that of others. Because God has given each of us free will in making choices, rebellious children often find themselves in situations that pose spiritual, mental and physical danger therefore adding "sin to sin".

Mother wrote in her journal, **"We must take God's commands seriously. It is not enough to know His word; we must follow it and apply it to our daily activities and decisions."**

Dear Lord, Thank you for the truth in Your Word that blesses us spiritually, physically and mentally. Help us to follow your commands and apply them to our daily life. Amen

Isaiah 40:29

He gives power to the weak, and to those who have no might He increases strength.

Our son was born with severe and multiple handicaps. My powerlessness overwhelmed and depressed me. The prayers of others carried me for the first years as I worked through the anger I felt at God for allowing the situation.

The anger led to outbursts which led to guilt and the guilt kept me from praying. I was tired from lack of sleep and a wimpy mess overall.

At two o'clock one morning as I sat rocking a screaming baby, I decided that I was all alone. Finally I shook my fist in the air and yelled, "You are not there! If you were, I wouldn't be in this mess!"

For a split second I felt a void in my spirit and bleakness as if He said, "Let me show you what it's like if I'm not here."

In that nanosecond my faith was strengthened, but I still face situations that test it. When those times come, I grab my Bible and run to Him. I hide under His wings until my doubts subside and my strength returns.

In her journal Mother wrote, "**We may have strong faith, but we also have weak spots and that is when temptation usually strikes. We must strengthen and protect our weak areas.**"

Dear Lord, Make me as strong today as I need to be. Amen

God Watches Over Us

I just read *Orphan Train*, by Christina Baker Kline.

The book parallels the lives of a wealthy elderly woman, Vivian, and Molly, a teenage foster child. It seems unlikely that the two would have anything in common, but when Molly must complete fifty hours of community service for stealing a book from the library an unexpected bond develops between the two women.

As it turns out, Vivian was one of thousands of children who were sent from New York City to the Midwest on orphan trains from 1824 through 1929. Through the author's use of a dual narrative, we gain insight into the similarities of their childhoods decades apart.

When the author writes, "It is a pitiful kind of childhood to know that no one loves you or is taking care of you." She's expressing a feeling both characters know too well.

Monday night our book club gathered but instead of discussing the book, we invited a friend whose father and uncle rode an orphan train.

Our friend told a moving story of a five year old that, after a station stop, was left to ride the train alone after a family chose his older brother but didn't want him.

Riding to the very last station, the boy and all the other children who were left on the train were taken in by a doctor and her husband in a small rural Nebraska town.

He stayed with them for two years and one day she told him they were going to see another family who had a horse for him. The doctor took him to the family that would eventually adopt him.

Realizing the child's musical talent, his new parents provided lessons and demanded he practice. He became and accomplished musician, and as a young man during World War II became a member of General Patton's band.

He married and eventually became a high school band director.

Our friend made a point of reading *Orphan Train* before coming to tell his father's story, and he posed this question, **"So is it just human nature to believe that things happen for a reason – to find some shred of meaning even in the worst experiences?"** and followed it with this observation,

"My father was a man of faith and I believe he would say that the hand of God was in the whole experience from being orphaned in New York to being adopted in Nebraska. That being said, his experience left a mark so deep that he was unable to share it with us until four years before he died."

Mother wrote in her journal, **"The Lord watches over us in all the different places, and He will not allow even one trial that is too much for us."**

As He watched over the children on the Orphan Train, I pray He will continue to protect and guide all of our children.

Isaiah 41:10

Fear not for I am with you. Be not dismayed for I am your God. I will strengthen you. Yes, I will help you. I will uphold you in my righteous right hand.

An antonym for fear is courage, and an antonym for dismayed is comforted. God doesn't want us to be fearful or dismayed. He wants us to be courageous and comforted because He will be our help in every situation.

At twenty-seven, my husband became the head football coach at Ottawa University in Kansas. We packed up three kids and all our worldly goods and head for the Midwest. The move was an important step of faith that led to many blessings that were ours to claim, but only if we trusted Him.

The enemy often tried to scare and dismay us, but we knew God was with us.

In her journal Mother wrote, **"It isn't enough to get off on the right foot in building our marriage, career or church on God's principles. We must remain faithful to God to the end. He must be in control from start to finish."**

Dear Lord, Thank you for the courage and comfort You promise us. Help us be wise and look to You when we are fearful or dismayed. Amen

Isaiah 43: 18-19

Do not remember the former things, nor consider the things of old. Behold I will do a new thing. Now it shall spring forth. Shall you not know it? I will make a road in the wilderness and rivers in the desert.

One of the sharpest weapons in the devil's bag of tricks is guilt. If he can nudge us into ruminating on mistakes and disappointments in our past, he has a chance to use the guilt to separate us from God and His plans for our future.

Learn from your mistakes, but don't dwell on them or fall into the snare of guilt and separation from the One who desires the very best for you.

New opportunities require thoughtful consideration. Every day is a gift He can use to move you forward so it is important to talk it out with God before seeking anyone else's advice. He is always doing new things.

Mother wrote in her journal, **"Determine if the result of following someone's advice will make improvements in your life and give a positive solution or direction. Advice is only helpful if it is consistent with God's standard and moves you forward"**.

Dear Lord, Thank you for the new things you have in store for us. Help us let go of the past and move forward. Amen

Made in the USA
Lexington, KY
09 July 2015